Art goes underground

Art goes

EDITED BY GÖRAN SÖDERSTRÖM

Translated from the Swedish by
LAURIE THOMPSON

underground

ART IN THE STOCKHOLM METRO

LETTURA
Box 1308
S-171 25 Solna · Sweden

Front cover: Sculpture by Hertha Hillfon at Danderyds Sjukhus
station. Small picture: "Rainbow" by Åke Pallarp and Enno Hal-
leck at Stadion station
Back cover: "The Golosches of Fortune" by Sigvard Olsson at
Rådhuset station. Part of Helga Henschen's work of art at Tensta
station. "Newton's Apple" by Lennart Mörk at Tekniska Högsko-
lan station
Title page: Relief by Hertha Hillfon at Danderyds Sjukhus station.
Photo by Per Bergström
Cover photos by Hans Ekestang
Graphic Design: Johan Ogden, Förlagsateljén
Translation: Laurie Thompson
© 1985, 1988 by the authors and the Committee for Stockholm
Research
Printed by Centraltryckeriet AB, Borås, 1988

ISBN 91-85-50040-2

Contents

Preface

A bustling communications system, a modern and efficient transport network carrying almost a million passengers every working day, and at the same time the world's longest art gallery, open more or less round the clock. Such is the subterranean face of Stockholm, the underground railway. In 58 of the network's 99 stations, 159 artists worked for thirty years to produce works of art for the underground. Their work ranges from a single painting to a complete cave station, and was carried out during the years 1956–1985; the total artistic environments created under ground are the result of the biggest monumental art project in Sweden, and perhaps in Europe, since the war.

When the Stockholm City Council decided to proceed with plans to build the underground on 16 June, 1941, many people shook their heads. Discussions had been taking place on and off since the turn of the century, it is true, and several commissions of enquiry had reported on the subject; even so, no town as small as Stockholm had ever decided to build an underground railway. In 1941, the population of Stockholm had risen to 600,000. Budapest was the first city on the European mainland to acquire an underground railway, and when it was inaugurated in 1896, the population there was 700,000. Around 1957 there were about 100 cities in the world larger than Stockholm, but of those only 20 had an underground. At that time, there were 35 cities in Europe with a million or more inhabitants, but only eleven of them had an underground. By 1957, the population of Stockholm had risen to 800,000 inhabitants.

The decision to proceed with the underground in 1941 was a challenge to engineering techniques, and to the city's finances. We now know that both challenges were met, and that the decision was far-sighted. Stockholm's town planners, the Highways Commission and Stockholm Tramways Ltd, made a great success of the venture, which was extremely important for the development of the Stockholm region in the post-war years.

In 1971, the Stockholm County Council assumed responsibility for public transport, and hence also for further expansion of the underground. Artistic decoration of the underground stations, initiated by the City Council in 1955, has been overseen by the Stockholm Transport Art Advisory Council as a sub-committee of the regional council, and also by Stockholm Transport Ltd. The Södra Järva line was opened in the autumn of 1985, and only minor extensions of the network are envisaged for the foreseeable future. The Committee for Stockholm Research, the Stockholm County Council and Stockholm Transport therefore considered it important to summarize the development of the architectural and artistic design of the underground over the last fifty years or more by publishing this book. Since the art featured in the Stockholm underground has aroused great interest internationally, the Stockholm Transport Art Advisory Council has decided to produce this edition in English. I would like to express my gratitude to the various authors, most of whom have themselves taken an active part in bringing art underground over many years, for their contributions, and to the publishers for their helpful cooperation.

Lilian Grassman
Chairman

Foreword

One could say, paradoxically, that art in the Stockholm underground is a product of 1968. Paradoxically, because art first found its way under ground more than a decade earlier. The truth of the matter is, however, that ideas about the role of art in society propounded during the radical years at the end of the 1960s were basically the same as those behind the project to bring art into the underground—the concept of democratizing art, art as an everyday item of goods, and the view of the artist not as a divinely inspired prophet but rather a worker like everyone else, working for the good of the community as a whole.

Needless to say, these ideas are much older than that. August Strindberg argued against drawing-room art in his radical writings from the 1880s, and appealed for art to be regarded as a utility aimed at people in general: "Art must not continue to be designed for the elite if it is to justify its existence and be more than an ephemeral phenomenon." In the early years after the Russian revolution, radical Russian artists worked enthusiastically for the revolutionary cause, often with various forms of applied art which may not always have been comprehensible to the people for whom it was created. One could perhaps see the magnificently decorated underground stations in Moscow, dating from the 1930s, as a reflection of this aim of bringing art to the people—even though the art to be seen there was no longer radical but more of a return to the pompous styles of an earlier age. The Moscow underground was frequently invoked in the early discussions on art in the Stockholm underground, both as a model and as a frightening example of how not to do it.

Art in the Stockholm underground is utility art, in the true meaning of the term, especially in the new stations built from about 1970 onwards. The artistic design makes it possible to use much simpler and cheaper fittings in the underground stations, and at the same time gives individual stations a characteristic and recognizable identity. The different impression made by each station acts as a substitute for the stimulus given by the constantly changing environment on the surface, and makes the long journeys which most passengers have to undertake through deep rock tunnels day in, day out, bearable. Art which has served its usefulness and looks shabby, such as the "loose pictures" at Slussen and Mariatorget, can be removed and replaced by something new.

The subterranean stations designed as an artistic whole have been received very positively by the general public, in all probability more so than any previous manifestation of public art in Sweden; on the other hand, individual works of art nouveau in suburban stations still seem to leave many people confused or indignant. Underground art thus throws an interesting light on the ability and desire of the man in the street to react to a work of art. In recent years the choice of artists has also undergone a marked democratization process, even if the democracy has had to be representative, for obvious reasons.

Despite the radical nature of art in the underground, it has never led to political disagreement. Even when the first decision was made by the City Council in 1956, agreement on the matter crossed all party boundaries, and it has continued that way among all the politically elected representatives over the years. Underground art is the result of creative cooperation between artists and architects, engineers, administrators and elected representatives. Writing the history of art in the underground, therefore, means that many names must be named and the course of many events described.

Indeed, this very book is the result of cooperation between many contributors, most of them most accurately described as "participating observers" for many years while work to bring art underground was proceeding. The historical account is based on minutes, statements, letters and other written documents, supplemented by interwiews and personal memories. We have not considered it useful to burden our account with detailed source references or footnotes, and beg the reader to make allowances for the possibility of facts and recollections being interpreted in different ways, and of memories being selective and not always reliable.

The main authors for the various chapters in the book are as follows: *Introduction* Göran Söderström, *Technical Description* Bertil Linnér, *Architecture* Per H Reimers and Göran Söderström, *Prelude* Mailis Stensman, *The T-Centralen Competition, The Days of von Heland, The Stockholm Transport Art Advisory Council and the New Underground* Göran Söderström with the assistance of Juhan Grünfeldt, Bertil Linnér and Mailis Stensman, *Economy, Maintenance, Graffiti* Juhan Grünfeldt, Lennart Nyström and Göran Söderström, *The Underground and Public Art* Mailis Stensman. *The Stations in Words and Pictures* Mailis Stensman. The chief photographers were Hans Ekestang and Göran Fredriksson; the latter was also responsible for the series of pictures in Chapter 1. The overview of art and artists was made by Eva-Britt Gullers. The editor and the editorial committee are responsible for the final version of the text and the choice of pictures, but Mailis Stensman is responsible for the *Prelude* and *The Underground and Public Art*. The book was designed by Johan Ogden, and the publisher's editor was Siv Båvenholm, Liber Förlag.

Göran Söderström

Introduction

What is an underground railway? An efficient transport system which whisks harrassed city dwellers along under streets paralysed by traffic jams, a suburban line where commuters spend a large part of their active lives travelling to and from work, a warm refuge for teenagers at odds with society, drunkards, drug-addicts and all the other late-night clientele of a big city, a concert hall for street musicians of varying quality, a must for provincial tourists. The underground, the metro, the subway—call it what you will: it is a special feature of a big city with an appeal all of its own. It is often a hard world, as in New York where travellers tend to avoid cars with no guards on duty, or in Berlin where the stations around Bahnhof Zoo are crawling with drug addicts and prostitutes of both sexes. Or on the Stockholm underground, heading for a concert at "Oasen" in Rågsved: "It's a terrific feeling getting on the train as everybody else gets off—we frighten 'em to death. Everybody has a bag full of booze, and sits there knocking it back, chewing the fat and having a ball. We were a great gang, punks and punk rockers at the Gallerian station, us and the skins and the rest of 'em. We were set on beating up the mods. There was a terrific atmosphere, something special, all of us going to concerts, 40 or 50 at a time." (Interview with Johan, aged 18, inmate in a detention centre.)

Every metropolitan underground system has a character of its own. The Tube in London, the mother of them all, is precisely what its nickname suggests: a big, soul-less tube where the modern coaches have to fit into its rounded contours. The Moscow underground is a high-tech traffic system linking splendid but rather dull subterranean waiting rooms, resplendent in marble and with dazzling chandeliers. The remarkably attractive network in overcrowded Mexico City wends its way between excavations of ancient ruined temples, and boasts a well thought-out system of symbols for the various stations and lines, designed for illiterates. The new underground railways in Vienna, Munich and San Francisco display an elegance seemingly untouched by modern-day vandalism. Beneath the old Stadtmitte, the West Berlin U-Bahn clatters through eerily deserted and decrepit stations where the only sign of life is the

Weekday passengers at T-Centralen.

occasional East German border guard, strangely remote in the pale light.

The Grande Dame of underground railways, the Métropolitain in Paris, is predominantly a transport system for the inner city; only recently have lines been extended into the inner suburbs. On the other hand, the youngest sister of the Paris metro, the Helsinki network, is primarily a suburban line with only a few stations in the city centre. The same principle applied when the Stockholm underground was opened in 1933; it was in fact a series of subterranean stations on the tram line leading to the southern suburbs along the route Slussen—Skanstull. As is true even today of the modern underground system in Cologne, for example, the "trains" were in fact ordinary tramcars using overhead cables.

Around the turn of the century, it was thought that a town should have a population of at least a million to justify building an underground railway: a proposal to create an underground was discussed seriously in Stockholm despite the fact that the population at that time was only about 350,000. Various proposals were put forward over the years, and after long drawn-out discussions the local authority eventually decided in 1941 to build a genuine underground railway, having jumped the gun with the underground train routes to the southern suburbs in 1930—33. It was not possible to start building until the end of the Second World War, in August, 1945; the first line, which was in fact no more than an upgrading of the original tram routes to "underground standards", was opened in 1950. Two years later an extension westwards was brought into operation between Hötorget and Lindhagensgatan, and the "connecting route" Slussen—Hötorget was opened in 1957.

The first underground lines were entirely within the boundaries of the city of Stockholm, and both built and financed by the city. The company responsible for urban transport was still SS, i e AB Stockholms Spårvägar (Stockholm Tramways Ltd), a municipal company pure and simple. This was natural enough, since most of the population of the Stockholm region still lived inside the city boundaries. The increasing demands on space in the city centre for

Street musicians under ground.

administrative and commercial purposes, however, together with a growing need for accommodation and commercial premises, meant that future expansion must extend into the areas around Stockholm itself.

In June 1965, a committee made up of experts from various local authorities and Stockholms Spårvägar produced an overall plan for an underground network designed to interconnect with bus services and local trains run by Swedish Railways and form a comprehensive public transport system for Greater Stockholm (*Stockholms län*). Negotiations took place with the various other councils concerned, and it was decided that from 1971 onwards the Stockholm County Council should accept overall responsibility for the building and operation of the underground network in Greater Stockholm, assisted by special state subsidies.

In 1964 the old tramway routes leading to the south-western suburbs were turned into an underground line, the so-called "second line", and the following year it was extended diagonally in a north-easterly direction as far as Östermalmstorg, and continued to Ropsten in 1967. The "third line" came into being in 1975, the Järva line linking the newly built suburbs in the north-west of the city. The original intention was that this third line should be called the Nacka Line and continued diagonally southwards, with Kungsträdgården as the big central station: this explains why the Kungsträdgården station was built on a much more splendid scale than is justified by the small number of passengers using it today. The last of the big lines, Södra Järvabanan (the Southern Järva Line), was opened in 1985 to extend the Järva Line between the Västra Skogen and Rinkeby stations. All three lines cross in the city centre at T-Centralen.

Today, the underground railway consists of 110 km of double track and 99 stations. Every day some 1.3 million people travel into the centre of Stockholm, and of these about 700,000 go by public transport, approximately 400,000 using the underground. It has been calculated that on a normal weekday, about 700,000 passengers use the Stockholm underground at some point.

Technical description

Rock tunnels

The most significant development to take place over the years the underground system was being constructed concerns the building method used. The table distinguishes between methods used on each of the three lines, and shows how more and more reliance was placed on rock tunnels. There are various reasons for this development.

A rock tunnel can be constructed from start to finish without affecting existing buildings or normal activities on the surface. A tunnel constructed from the surface usually means considerable disruption during the building period. An example of this is the tunnel under Sveavägen in central Stockholm, on line one. For several years this street was a cluttered and noisy building site, resulting in widespread disruption, and businessmen with premises in adjacent buildings demanded compensation for revenue lost due to difficulties customers experienced in gaining access to their shops. By way of contrast, when the south-west tunnel was being built under Södermalm, all tunnels were rock tunnels and the only disruption was caused by the construction of the ticket offices and entrances from street level. Other advantages of rock tunnels are the greater scope they provide for meeting the technical requirements of the railway, and the fact that they can comparatively easily be adapted for civil defence purposes.

One of the main reasons, and indeed perhaps the main reason for building rock tunnels is of course the relatively low cost. Thanks to the generally sound quality of the rock in the Stockholm area and the high level of rock-blasting technology in Sweden, the cost of building rock tunnels has not increased at the same rate as building costs generally, despite continually rising wages. A twin-track rock tunnel, for instance, with all the necessary reinforcement and water-proofing works, costs about one fifth as much as a concrete tunnel using the old methods.

Most of the more recent stations have been built as rock tunnel stations, but it is not so easy to produce comparative costs for concrete and rock tunnel stations as it is for the tunnels themselves,

Line		Length in kilometres					Length as %			
		Total	Rock tunnel	Concrete tunnel	Bridge or viaduct	Open track	Rock tunnel	Concrete tunnel	Bridge or viaduct	Open track
Line 1	Hässelby strand – Lindhagensgatan	13,0	0,6	0,3	1,5	10,6	5	2	11	82
	Lindhagensgatan – Gullmarsplan	8,4	1,6	4,9	1,2	0,7	19	58	14	9
	Gullmarsplan – Farsta strand	8,3	0,5	0,1	1,0	6,7	6	1	12	81
	Gullmarsplan – Hagsätra	8,1	–	–	0,9	7,2	–	–	11	89
	Skärmarbrink – Bagarmossen	4,0	–	–	0,7	3,3	–	–	18	82
Line 1	Total	41,8	2,7	5,3	5,3	28,5	6	13	13	68
Line 2	Ropsten – T-Centralen	4,9	3,8	0,3	0,5	0,3	78	6	10	6
	Östermalmstorg – Mörby C	8,7	7,5	0,9	0,2	0,1	86	11	2	1
	Slussen – Fruängen	8,4	5,1	0,5	0,7	2,1	61	6	8	25
	Liljeholmen – Vårberg	9,6	5,0	0,9	0,2	3,5	52	10	2	36
	Vårberg – Norsborg	8,7	4,6	0,7	1,5	1,9	53	8	17	22
Line 2	Total	40,3	26,0	3,3	3,1	7,9	64	8	8	20
Line 3	Kungsträdgården – Västra Skogen	5,1	4,7	0,4	–	–	92	8	–	–
	Västra Skogen – Hallonbergen	3,8	3,3	0,5	–	–	87	13	–	–
	Hallonbergen – Akalla	6,7	3,9	0,6	1,5	0,7	58	9	22	11
	Västra Skogen – Rinkeby	7,2	7,2	–	–	–	100	–	–	–
	Rinkeby – Hjulsta	2,8	2,7	0,1	–	–	96	4	–	–
	Hallonbergen – Rinkeby	2,6	2,3	0,3	–	–	88	12	–	–
Line 3	Total	28,2	24,1	1,9	1,5	0,7	85	7	5	3
Lines 1–3	Whole underground network	110,3	52,8	10,5	9,9	37,1	48	10	9	33

since many other factors are involved: the design of the ticket office area, for example, the extent of pedestrian subways, the number of lifts and escalators and their lengths, and so on. As a rough guide, however, it is worth noting that Hjulsta station, a rock tunnel station, cost about one quarter as much as the one at Danderyds Sjukhus, a concrete station.

A disadvantage of rock tunnel stations is that most of them are located a comparatively long way below street level. On line three, the average station depth is 25–30 m, which means they need expensive escalators and lifts. Nevertheless, the overall financial profile is such that it is advantageous to exploit to the full the sound bedrock on which Stockholm stands.

Geology

The bedrock under Stockholm was formed some two million years ago. It is often called greystone, which is a collective term for various types of stone occurring in the bedrock. The rock consists mainly of gneiss, granite and amphibolite, and the commonest type of granite is so-called Stockholm granite, which is very strong when

Stadion station,
From *The Stockholm Underground 1975.*

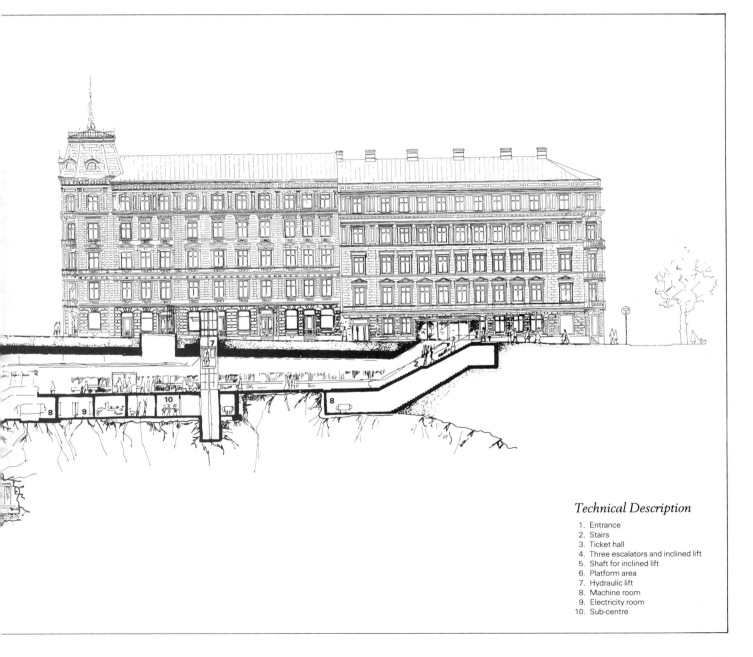

Technical Description

1. Entrance
2. Stairs
3. Ticket hall
4. Three escalators and inclined lift
5. Shaft for inclined lift
6. Platform area
7. Hydraulic lift
8. Machine room
9. Electricity room
10. Sub-centre

not weathered. The state of the bedrock in which the tunnels have been made has varied considerably—it must be remembered that the whole network of tunnels is comparatively near the surface, which means problems such as poor rock covering in parts, and subsoil water leakage. The condition of rock near the surface is usually worse than that deeper down.

Rock reinforcement — sprayed concrete

Even if the rock is generally good in quality, a degree of reinforcement is needed in some places. When work started on the underground railway, the only available strengthening method was the use of concrete arches cast on site: about 100 of these were used when building the older Fridhemsplan station. Nowadays rock riveting frequently occurs as well.

During the 1960s, sprayed concrete started to be generally used for strengthening rock tunnels and all tunnels built during the last 25 years have had a layer of sprayed concrete at least 30 mm thick in the roof. In stations, the sprayed concrete has been about 80 mm thick and is also reinforced. A plastic tube drainage system is inserted between the rock and the sprayed concrete so as to avoid water leakage in the tunnel.

Planning

SL (Stockholm Transport) have been responsible for planning the underground rail system, and the Stockholm Highways Commission has been used as consultants for the static constructions. The Stockholm Highways Commission has also been engaged by SL for the actual building work, and they have done some of the work themselves but contracted out the rest. There has been cooperation with specialists from the contractors even at the planning and projection stages, when various methods have been discussed for injection, rock blasting etc. SL's architectural section was responsible for designing and fitting the stations, and the architects frequently worked together with artists on the artistic design of stations.

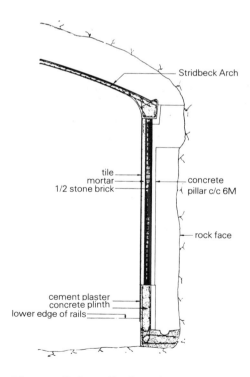

The so-called Stridbeck Arch.

24

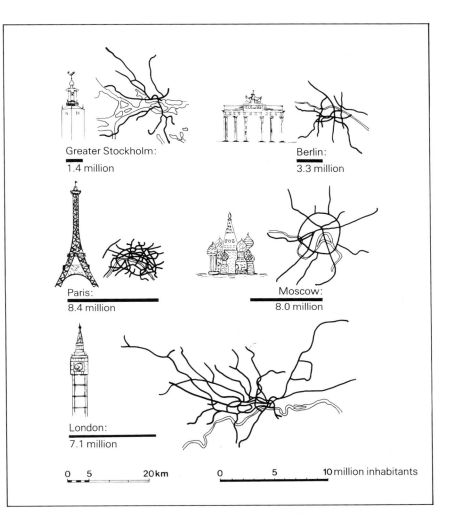

Greater Stockholm:
1.4 million

Berlin:
3.3 million

Paris:
8.4 million

Moscow:
8.0 million

London:
7.1 million

0   5   20 km   0   5   10 million inhabitants

Length of underground network in relation to population, 1980. From The Stockholm Underground 1975. Technical Description.

Construction of the tracks

The underground railway has a very high traffic load of up to 22 million axle tons per section of track per year. Since traffic runs for roughly twenty hours per day, little time is available for maintenance work and this in turn means that maintenance costs are high. This makes it necessary to use track construction methods which guarantee a high level of technical performance at economical cost. Attention must also be paid to low sound levels and good working conditions in the tunnels. In Stockholm there is plenty of good-quality stone, especially granite, for making macadam, and so the tracks have been constructed conventionally with macadam ballast, in accordance with the requirements mentioned above. Nowadays concrete sleepers are used instead of the wooden ones used earlier. A comparative study has shown that exclusively concrete track would cost about 75% more than the conventional track used at present, and concrete tracks also have other disadvantages such as high sound levels, longer construction times, complicated track anchoring etc. The track width used on the underground is the so-called normal track width of 1,435 mm. The track is all-welded between the insulation joints for the signalling system. The rail weight is 50 kg/m.

Power supply and signalling system

The power supply for the underground is 750 volts direct current, fed from rectifier stations to a third rail, the so-called live rail. The rectifier stations are located in separate buildings and each one is fed by 30 kV 3-phase alternating current. The rectifier stations have a nominal effect of 5−6 MV, and they are approximately 2.2 km apart.

The Stockholm underground uses a cabin signalling system with automatic train control. There are three speed commands, and the speed limit is indicated at every point: the permitted speed depends on the distance to the preceding train or other obstacles, such as points. The automatic train control system applies the brakes if a train should happen to exceed the speed limit indicated by the cabin signal

In theory, the signalling system assumes a train every 90 seconds, but in practice the frequency of trains is one every other minute, due to station stops.

Of course, it is not possible to do away altogether with fixed signals on the track, which are needed for such obstacles as points. There are four signal boxes from which train routes can be coordinated.

Stations

Of the 99 stations 45 are located underground, and most of them are blasted into the rock. Over the years there has been an interesting trend regarding the form the stations take.

Standard comparison between concrete stations from the 1930s, 1970s and 1980s.

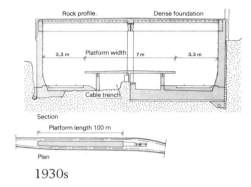

1930s

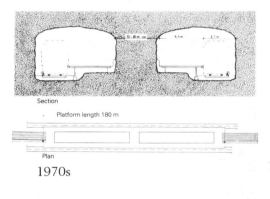

1970s

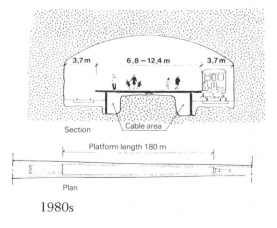

1980s

During the 1950s station tunnels were excavated with a section of 50 m², and constructed in concrete with concrete pillars, concrete arches and generally brick walls between the pillars. The walls were usually clad with ceramic material and the floors were made of ceramic tiles or cement mosaic.

Stations built during the 1960s were basically similar in construction, but the materials used for wall cladding varied considerably. Some stations had walls covered in glazed brick or various forms of concrete, while others used enamelled sheet metal or glass prisms.

The disadvantage of this type of station is that it takes a comparatively long time to apply the decorative finish, and while such work is taking place it is often necessary to shut down all traffic in the relevant tunnel. Efforts were thus made to find a different method which would speed up the actual fitting and if possible reduce installation costs. This led to the idea of "cave stations". There are various kinds of cave station, and the early ones were made as follows.

The excavated chamber was thoroughly drained and treated with sprayed concrete, and then a light suspended ceiling of aluminium and steel was hung in place. The ceiling was made of extruded aluminium and metal mesh, and parts of the walls were also clad in wire mesh. Sound absorbent material was placed on top of the suspended ceiling, and under the edges of the platforms.

A development of the cave station format was used on line three, in that the ceiling was replaced by lengthwise and crosswise girders of expanded metal mesh containing mineral wool for sound absorption.

Most of the cave stations have a pillar of unexcavated rock on the platforms containing a crosswise tunnel connecting the two sides of the platform. Four of the new stations which came into operation in August 1985, however, are rather different. These stations, known as "trumpet stations", have one central platform with no pillar. At the end where the escalators and lifts terminate, the roof span is about 22 m, but the chamber grows narrower and measures only 14 m or so at the other end. The advantage of this design is that

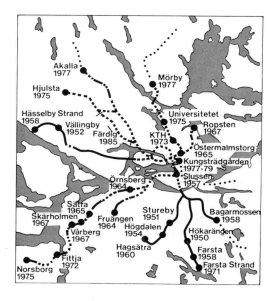

Extensions to the underground network.

Rådhuset station, with a pedestrian subway between Kungsholmsgatan and Hantverkargatan.

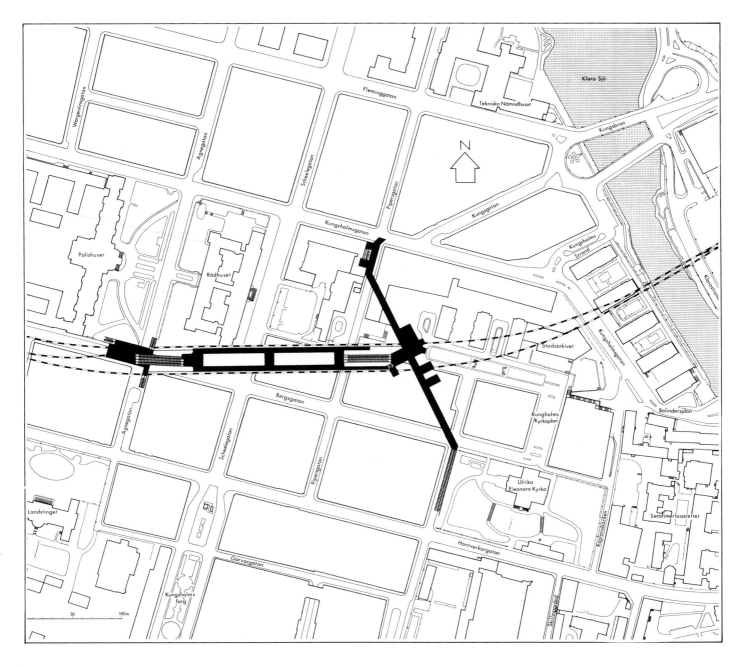

there is a good view over the whole length of the platform, and the walls are inaccessible for graffiti or other possible interference. Instead of sound absorbers hanging in the roof, the trumpet stations have so-called "milieu girders" along the sides of the platforms only, suspended from cantilevers attached to pillars placed centrally on the platforms.

One of the big technical advantages of rock stations over their predecessors is that the rough rock face diffuses sound, and this together with the sound absorption devices creates a pleasantly low-noise environment. The larger chambers also make rock stations less draughty than the earlier type of station.

When the Stockholm underground was planned, escalators were a relatively new concept, and hence only the deep stations in the town centre were provided with escalators. There were no lifts at all in the early stations. Among the reasons for this were reports from foreign underground systems suggesting that lifts were easily vandalized or damaged, and the fact that they were not very reliable. Nevertheless, lifts became increasingly common in underground stations thanks to pressure from various organizations for the disabled, and from other categories of passengers such as those with prams and push-chairs.

Nowadays all new stations have lifts linking platforms with street level, although in some cases, when local conditions allow, there might be a gentle ramp instead of a lift. The aim is that passengers should be able to go from street level to platform level without needing to use staircases or escalators. All deep stations are provided with three escalators, but the number might vary in stations that are not so deep, or in the area between the ticket offices and the street. Escalators are not normally installed when the difference in level is less than 5 m.

Much attention was paid to other measures aimed at helping the disabled, such as the special markings along platform edges and on staircases for passengers who do not see so well.

Vandalism in stations and in coaches is a difficult problem, and assuming it could not be eliminated completely, care was taken to

Application of sprayed concrete.

use material difficult to vandalize and easy to replace, as far as possible. Wherever glass is used, for instance, it is largely chemically hardened laminated glass. The shaping of walls with sprayed concrete as described above is a deterrent to scribbling and graffiti. Nevertheless, in spite of all precautions the cost of damage due to vandalism is unfortunately very high.

Future building works

Generally speaking, the oldest parts of the underground are now some 35 years old (and indeed, the first section is 50 years old), which means that the stations in particular are in need of rebuilding and modernizing. There are plans to instal lifts in the older stations, and for their general modernization—some of them are nearing the end of their life span from a technical point of view.

After the completion of work to extend the line between Västra Skogen and Rinkeby, the following projects are due for action. A 2.5 km extension from Bagarmossen to Skarpnäck, involving one new and one rebuilt station, should be ready for traffic around 1994, and there may be another extension running from Akalla to the Hansta district. A branch line from Alvik to Bromma airport is another possible project, but no further decisions have yet been made concerning any more extensions or branches.

Architecture

The earliest and biggest underground networks were created in a spirit of technology and the engineers were given free rein. Nowadays such systems are admired first and foremost as technological innovations which still work, and they bear the unmistakable stamp of the age in which they were built. They are often a hotch-potch of several individual parts combined to form a whole transport system, and incorporate many makeshift measures.

Underground railways serving city centers, especially the early ones, are often only a short way below the surface and are linked with the road system above ground, with consequent limitations as far as design and space are concerned. The classical building method was to excavate open shafts in the streets, and then to make load-bearing constructions in steel or concrete just below street level, and at certain intervals such shafts were turned into stations. This method was used for the subterranean parts of the Stockholm underground which came into being during the 1930s and 1950s. It was only when the central Klara district was razed and rebuilt that stations on the section of the underground running diagonally across the area could be allowed to influence planning on the surface. Apart from that, a characteristic of the Stockholm underground is that from the very start it was designed as a coherent whole, and the planners had the foresight to prepare the way by such means as for instance reserving sites and building the St Eriksbron bridge in the 30s.

In an international context, it is fair to say that the Stockholm underground has developed at a modest pace. Expertise has been acquired and nurtured locally, and largely within the city's own Highways Commission and its own transport organizations. These organizations have been responsible for the architectural design, and the architects have been able to identify with the client.

Completely new underground railways are currently being built all over the world: inevitably, they are great national projects involving billions of pounds, and thousands of experts are busy incorporating the latest technical innovations. Those responsible, assuming they are not short of money, are able to call in international experts and aim to build the most advanced system of all, from both operating and design points of view. What used to take several decades to construct can now be achieved in one. The result is an international style; only if he is lucky can the architect manage to assimilate something of the local atmosphere and culture in the short time at his disposal, and give the underground a character which harmonizes with the rest of the town.

Despite the severe restrictions, the design of the earlier stations on the Stockholm underground reflects the characteristic style of contemporary Swedish architecture, but it was when the network was extended to the new suburbs of Vällingby and Farsta in the 1950s and 1960s that international interest was aroused. Then came the rock excavations and cave architecture, when the Stockholm bedrock was exploited in a way which gave the Stockholm underground a character of its own. Another special characteristic is the involvement of artists, which started as early as the 1950s but blossomed out into something unique in combination with the cave architecture. The Stockholm underground inspired international exhibitions arranged by the Swedish Institute, the Stockholm County Council and Stockholm Transport (SL), which helped to make Swedish rock excavation techniques known abroad, and to bring about the cooperation between engineers, architects and artists so typical of the Stockholm network.

There has been a tendency among those involved in building the underground in the 1950s not to acknowledge its origins in the Slussen—Skanstull line, one reason being that its trains were powered by overhead cables. Nevertheless, the stations and the subterranean sections were built to the metro standard, and were in fact the model for the whole of the first underground line.

The part of the line which did not run through rock was constructed in accordance with the so-called Berlin method, that is, the load-bearing sections were of steel and partly visible. Typical of the stations Södra Bantorget and Ringvägen, nowadays called Medborgarplatsen and Skanstull, were the row of painted steel pillars down the centre, and open cavities between the roof beams. The walls

were clad in frost-proof tiles of uniform colour and standard size. The upper hall had somewhat darker tiles in pastel shades, glazed ticket booths and glazed swing doors. "Typical of thirties transport architecture in their sober objectivity," according to the art critic Gotthard Johansson's assessment of the two stations in 1942. Soon after the first stage of the underground was complete, the architect responsible for those stations, Holger Blom, at that time attached to the Highways Commission, drew up detailed plans for the buildings underneath the famous cross road Slussen. Designed for pedestrians, they had walkways in various colours and little shops in functionalist style.

Particular attention was paid to the design of notice boards, lettering and advertising strips. The artist Kalle Lodén was responsible for these, and for the colour schemes. He also designed the original emblem, a large letter T in a circle, standing for the Swedish word for underground railway, *tunnelbana*. The carefully designed station environment was a model for future stations, but unfortunately the original stations were soon altered to their detriment. Rebuilding works in connection with the construction of the first branch line in the 1950s resulted in lower ceilings and changes in the colour schemes, notices, advertisements and lighting.

The stations Skanstull and Medborgarplatsen, together with Slussen and the stretch from T-Centralen to Fridhemsplan, are representative of the subterranean stations of the 1950s. Underground constructions were close to the surface and ceilings were generally moulded using the so-called "cut and cover" method. The first extension programme of the 1950s envisaged a line 80% above ground, but it was the subterranean stations which attracted most attention—partly because they were regarded as the "real" underground, and partly because they were located in the inner city. Architecturally, the opportunities they presented were very limited. The architect in overall charge of the inner city stations, Gunnar Lené of the Stockholm Highways Commission, described his work in the journal *Arkitektur* (Architecture) in 1953: "The biggest problem for an architect has been to get the dimensions right and to plan

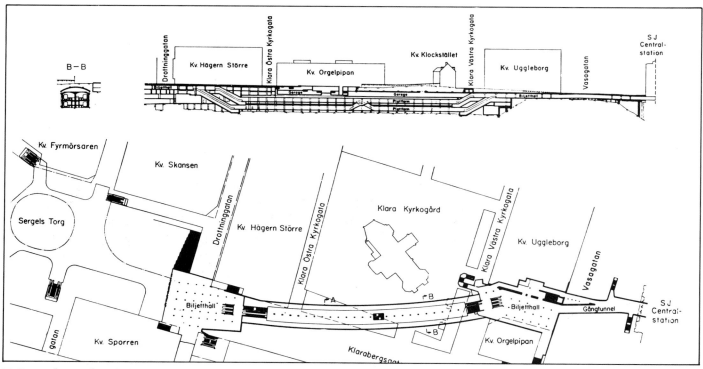

T-Centralen in the 1950s.

the walkways and spaces passengers must traverse when walking to and from the trains. During the building stage the fascinating thing has been the sheer scale of the struggle to overcome the rock and the masses of earth, and one is tempted to try and retain something which reflects that struggle. But rock drips, gravel causes dust, iron rusts: on the other hand, areas where people crowd together have to be bright and clean. What sticks in the mind are such things as stainless steel, non-slip stairways, and floor tiles and wall tiles in varying colours. The walls make the background for notices that are easy to read, for posters supplying colour and uplift, for boutiques which tempt the passer-by. The balance between these attractions must be such that clarity is not lost. – The comfort many people have expected is illustrated by the pictures reproduced in these pages, and the artistic experiences many people have sought after have been mundane commercial pleasures."

Nevertheless, efforts were made to vary the insides of the stations, and their designs were individual and very different, both in plan and in section, albeit for constructional reasons. The tiles are the same standard size as those used in the 1930s stations, but their

Odenplan station, 1984.

Hötorget station, 1984.

Hötorget station, 1984.

colour schemes reflect the variations in architectural design above ground and have been given life by so-called random distribution in several similar shades. As a result of their central locations and the special requirements dictated by their role in the overall city plan, the T-Centralen and Hötorget stations have an interesting sectional design in which special effects are achieved by vertical movements. The same applies to Slussen, but restrictions imposed by existing circumstances limited the scope to some extent. Skanstull, Medborgarplatsen, Rådmansgatan and St Eriksplan do not vary much in their internal appearance, and they are typical of stations built in steel or concrete directly underneath roadways. Fridhemsplan, however, is a deep rock station: columns of unexcavated rock divide the platform with tunnels joining the two sides of the platform at right angles to the rails. This type of construction became characteristic of subsequent subterranean stations. Odenplan is rather different. It has something of the old railway station atmosphere due to the fact that its roof is a single, stylish arch. The stairway leading down to it has a free-standing arched ceiling like a large concrete wing, and is a kind of sculpture designed by the skilful park architect, Erik Glemme.

Despite the sober objectivity and technology characteristic of the first expansion of the underground network, it was generally well received.

Typical of many of the stations is the effort put into the underground shopping centers. The trading laws of the 1950s allowed shops in "waiting areas for train passengers" to remain open in the evenings. They can also be seen as the maintaining of a tradition set by the transport architecture of the Slussen roundabout in the 1930s, and also in the first two underground stations.

People were afraid the stations would be dominated by crass commercialism and advertising, and this was one of the things which eventually led to proposals for artists to be involved in the designing of the underground. Once art got a toe-hold in the stations, it was received so enthusiastically, as in the case of T-Centralen for instance, that they threatened to burst from the sheer volume of artistic expression.

The surface stations built in the suburbs in the 1950s were characterized by modest architecture in the style of provincial railway stations or tram stops. Standards were not as rigorous as they are today. It was thought that escalators, for instance, should only be located inside the barriers so that they could be kept under observation by barrier staff; no lifts were installed, and this means that supplementary building work has to be carried out now. About half the stations were converted from old tram stops with no ticket booths and no protective roof, and alterations had to be made without stopping the traffic. The surface stations dating from the fifties are clear examples of architecture in which the building materials themselves were featured as a quality. Concrete, steel, glass, wood, Eternit, glazed tiles and asphalt, together with the uniformly simple architectural form, seemed so natural that it eventually came to be denigrated along with all so-called glass and concrete architecture. Peter Celsing was the chief architect in the Stockholm Tramways architectural office at that time, and it is quite possible to see parallels with his later work Kulturhuset (The House of Culture) in Stockholm.

Since the architectural qualities derive from restraint as regards materials and colour, and austerity in design details and proportions, these stations, after thirty years of faithful service, are particularly

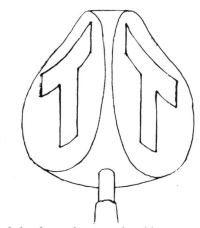

Sketch for the underground emblem.

Blackeberg station, 1952.

The ticket hall at Blackeberg station.

vulnerable to meddlesome "improvements" as regards building technology. Introducing artistic improvements as is now the fashion in the 1980s can also be seen as meddling and can easily develop into artistic prettification in the worst sense, even if in some cases, Bandhagen for instance, the artist managed to establish a rapport with the architect which enriched the station. In Vällingby the secondary passenger hall underneath the lines has created an irrational contrast, and that puts question marks against the brutalism conveyed by so much bad concrete architecture.

From an architectural point of view, the most representative examples of the fifties style are to be found in the surface stations, even though artistic details have been introduced. The idea of repeating certain details and variations on a theme reinforced the impression of travelling on a coherent network.

The inner city subterranean stations, then, were designed by architects working for the Highways Commission, while architects with Stockholm Tramways (SS) in general had to be satisfied with the more modest surface stations in the outskirts. However, some subterranean stations were also built outside the city center. One of Peter Celsing's finest achievements as a tramways architect is the great hall at Blackeberg station with its thin shell roof of reinforced concrete, where light enters both from underneath and from the large expanses of glass under the roof arches. The station at Vällingby, which is basically a bright courtyard surrounded by offices containing the entrance to a modest and partly open station, was designed by Magnus Ahlgren, who was in charge of the tramways architectural department from 1952 onwards.

With the T-Centralen and more especially Fridhemsplan showing the way, the advantages of excavating deeper into the rock began to be appreciated: disruption of surface traffic and demolition of buildings were avoided, and there was greater freedom in locating and designing stations. As a result, subterranean construction became dominant during the 1960s. The southwestern line is constantly emerging onto the surface before running underground once more, and in its northeasterly section as far as Ropsten it was natural to

The Odenplan station roof, 1953.

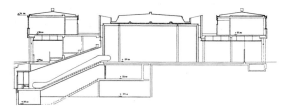
Plan for Vällingby station.

Model for Vällingby station.

44

Suburban station in the 1950s.

St Eriksplan station, 1953.

build underground. The surface stations vary considerably in design. There are minor variations in the typical fifties platform roof, but it is mainly the ticket halls which display most individuality. They became an expression of quite new architectural trends in the 1960s, and were integrated into the suburban centers. They were strongly influenced by the environment. Under the surface the Stridbeck arch (the concrete arch cast on site in the excavated area) became a strait-jacket, and design was governed by technical and financial considerations. Thus, several stations look more or less identical. One group with two entrances is formed by Mariatorget, Hornstull, Östermalmstorg, Karlaplan and Gärdet; another with only one entrance by Zinkensdamm, Mälarhöjden, Aspudden and Midsommarkransen. The similar construction of the stations meant that their individual character depended almost entirely on the contributions made by artists, and these developed increasingly in the direction of an integrated design—Siri Derkert's work on the Östermalmstorg station is one of the most interesting and most complete documentations of its time.

Bredäng station.

Moving walkway, Ropsten station.

*Pedestrian walkway to the bus station,
Ropsten station, 1960s.*

Variations in the material used on the walls and individual details from station to station gave the impression that overall architectural control was lacking. Glazed tiles, clinkers or brick, natural concrete, concrete and natural stone occurred in various combinations. The primary concern was durability, resistance to damage and ease of cleaning, in accordance with the functionalist creed described by Gunnar Lené in 1953. The only consistent details in the whole network were restricted to doors and barriers (which, incidentally, were made at Sigurd Lewerentz' factory IDESTA). Not even such an important aspect as notices were consistent. At Mälarhöjden, Hornstull and Östermalmstorg, all wall advertising was removed and replaced by artistic designs. Ever since the 1950s attempts had been made to solve the problem of draughts by installing shafts to equalize the pressure, but not much attention was paid to such functions as lighting and sound absorption.

All 1960s stations have escalators even outside the barriers, and in subterranean stations they are supplemented by either vertical or inclined lifts. Liljeholmen station even has a little mountain railway linking the station with the Nybohov area some 38 metres higher up. In general, the height of escalators varies between 4 and 20 metres. Although Östermalmstorg station is 38 metres below ground, there are two sets of escalators, with three in each.

Most of the 1960s surface stations were designed at a time when Sweden had never had it so good, and work coincided with large-scale building projects in the inner city and housing developments in the suburbs. In Skärholmen even the station became just one part of the big centre which was to be the commercial, social and cultural focus for the southwestern part of Greater Stockholm. The station was part of the terraced building which formed the kernel of the complex. Many of these suburban stations introduced pedestrian ramps as a means of assisting the disabled, and thus demonstrated their readiness to cooperate with user organizations. Concrete architecture became more and more dominant as a result of these ramps and the viaducts on which many of the stations were situated. Bredäng is an example of a station were a conscious effort was made

47

to use concrete architecture, and at Ropsten, the last of the 1960s stations, a moving walkway was installed in combination with pedestrian ramps. The moving walkway at Hjorthagen replaced the need for buses. The station also became one of the earliest expressions of "interchangeability", enabling passengers to transfer smoothly from buses and trains to the underground. The station is built partly on a viaduct, but the envisaged continuation by means of a bridge over to Lidingö and then on to Bogesundslandet and perhaps as far as the town of Vaxholm in the Stockholm archipelago has not yet materialized.

The extension of the southwestern line to Norsborg was part of the building programme for the 1970s. After the arrival of Michael Granit as chief architect in 1967, the series of architects responsible for the second line increased further, and in 1975 Per H Reimers was appointed to direct the architectural department of Stockholm Transport (SL). Other architects responsible for station design were Gunnar Lené, Magnus Ahlgren, Olle Blomqvist and Fred Giffen. The number of people involved obviously helps to explain the architectural variations on the second line, in contrast with line one, where Lené was responsible for the subterranean sections and Celsing and Ahlgren for the surface sections, and line three, where Granit and Reimers were entirely in charge.

The extension of the southwestern line continued to alternate between surface and underground stretches, and followed the same pattern as in the previous decade. The stations were integrated into suburban centres and housing estates which were generally planned and built at the same time as the underground extensions. Differences in level between upper and lower parts of the complex were reflected in the stations. This is particularly noticeable at Vårby Gård, were the various vertical movements between levels are achieved by means of pedestrian ramps, stairways, escalators and lifts. This gives the station a very special character as an example of transport architecture. It is also characterized by deliberate concrete architecture, and efforts have been made to exploit the form and texture of concrete. Hallunda and Norsborg, both situated under-

The excavated cave being worked on.

neath the Eriksberg complex and with large arrays of escalators and lifts up to the housing estates and pedestrian subway as well as to the pedestrian bridge over to the centre on the other side of Hallundavägen, are also examples of the type of transport architecture in which the underground station is the intermediary link.

The subterranean stations at Alby and Masmo play a similar role, but their chief interest is as subterranean stations and cave stations. In fact, Masmo was the first of the cave stations and the predecessor of the 20 cave stations built in the seventies on the Täby line (the extension of line 2 towards Mörby) and the Järva line (line 3).

A combination of determination on the part of the architects to express themselves, and improved rock excavation techniques, resulted in the cave stations of the 1970s. The basic idea behind the cave architecture was to break free from the concept of a concrete house inside a cavern, and to let the soft lines of the excavated cave contrast with the built-up or suspended constructional features.

Diffusion and dampening of noise was to be achieved by means of rough wall surfaces and suspended sound absorbers, while light and shade were to be important contrasting elements. The intention was also to complete the effect by having individual pictures or sculptures on the walls alongside the track, so that people were aware of things other than advertisements. Variations in colour were to give the stations an individual character.

However, this cavernous world opened the floodgates for the artists' imaginations, and something unique came into being in the Stockholm underground: a completely artificial environment in which the architectural ideas were reinforced and clarified by the input of artists. The various stations are linked by their common rock architecture and by certain design features which recur from station to station, but they are given an individual identity by their specific plan and the art they contain, giving colour and character, and enabling passengers to orientate themselves.

In many respects, Masmo station became a pilot project. Various fittings, roof designs, lighting, notices and even the colouring of sprayed concrete were tested in the rock chamber excavated for Stadshagen station, and the experience gained was put into practice in Masmo.

The fact that 20 new subterranean stations were going to be added to the underground network meant that the "house in the cave" concept could be put into question, and there was an opportunity to see whether the "cave world" would be accepted and thus give more scope.

Nevertheless, rock surfaces cannot simply be left as they are because of leakage and the danger of falling stones. They must be strengthened with the aid of rock bolts, injected and drained to prevent water leakage, and finally sprayed with a 5–7 cm thick layer of reinforced sprayed concrete. After being sprayed, the chamber walls follow the outlines of the rock, but edges and corners are softened. Damp, salt deposits and drips may occur here and there, but the tunnel is now acceptable as a place where a station can be built.

Stairway with metal mesh cladding, Masmo station.

On line 2, the cave stations have a latticed inner ceiling of extruded aluminium which was intended to conceal such visual blemishes as damp patches and salt deposits, and at the same time give a feeling of security and airiness. The ceiling and the lighting it incorporated emphasized the platforms as bright, colourful "islands" in the big, coherent "cave world".

Basically speaking, the station design tried out in Masmo involves the replacement of the earlier concrete shell and brick walls by metal mesh, that is, a lattice-like net of extruded metal which can be painted in bright colours. The rock face itself was to be treated with neutral dark-grey epoxy paint, so that the rock could be glimpsed vaguely behind the right-angled cladding on the ceiling and walls without appearing to be oppressive. The wall alongside the track would have a horizontal band with the name of the station, above which large areas of the rock face would be exposed behind and between advertising boards or similar boards with removable artistic decorations. The background colour of the rock face might vary from station to station, but within limits to ensure it retained its function as a neutral background. Sound-absorbing baf-

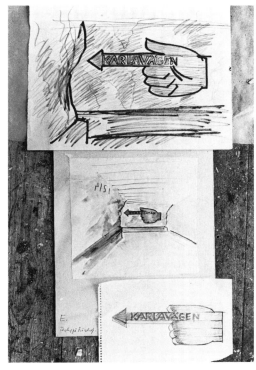

Enno Hallek: Sketches for exit signs to Karlavägen, Stadion station.

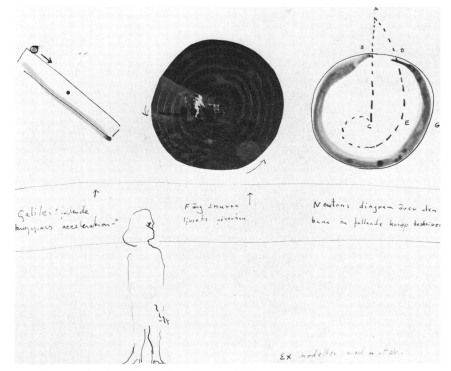

Lennart Mörk: Sketch for Tekniska Högskolan station.

fles and the necessary cables were to be hung behind the metal mesh ceiling. The information system was restrained and carefully thought out, a return to the high standards of the 1930s after the shortcomings of the intervening period, with black text on a white ground—which was to be the brightest surface in an area generally dimly lit.

At the sketching stage in 1970—71, a sculptor was engaged to join in discussions about materials and design, and building the model. At that time it was not clear whether any other artists would cooperate in designing the stations, which is why they hit upon the idea of boards with removable non-commercial art on the walls alongside the track: in that way the pictures exhibited, and hence the environment, could be changed just as old advertisements are replaced by new ones.

It was a hard task, persuading politicians, administrators, economists, technicians and transport officials to accept the new ideas for the stations. The biggest risk concerned safety, impenetrability and durability. It was also difficult to judge whether the caves would produce negative or claustrophobic reactions, and whether the simple design would be seen as a decline in environmental standards.

Passenger reaction could be assessed in Masmo, with regard to the cave design, the removable pictures, and the wall in the pedestrian tunnel where the wire mesh had been taken away and an informal picture painted directly onto the spray-concrete-coated wall by the artists Staffan Hallström and Lasse Andréasson. Meanwhile, Trafikens Konstnämnd (the Stockholm Transport Art Advisory Council) had been formed, and no one quite knew where the responsibility lay or what the possibilities were regarding cooperation with artists and sculptors on the artistic design of stations. The first decision of the council was to appoint Lennart Mörk to devise the artistic design for the Tekniska Högskolan station, and Åke Pallarp and Enno Hallek for the Stadion station. In many respects, these two stations became a "trial of strength", as Pallarp and Hallek wrote in KRO-bladet, 1974.

Decisions about artistic decorations were taken late compared with those on contractors. Proposals and alterations made by the artists had to be added to the contracting agreements after the building contractors had already been named. The architects were unpopular on all sides—with the artists for lack of understanding and interest, and with the building authorities for unnecessary complications which played straight into the hands of the contractors and meant unforeseen extra costs. "The sense of freedom we had experienced when first invited to submit sketches soon disappeared when we discovered that all the fittings had already been ordered through the contractors, for instance, the metal mesh which we did not want. Eventually, a compromise was agreed between us and Stockholm Transport: certain wall surfaces were uncovered, and the ceiling was taken away from the connecting tunnel", Pallarp and Hallek wrote in KRO-bladet.

In the Stadion and Tekniska Högskolan stations there is a large concrete plinth all the way along where the rock wall meets the platform, and this supports the metal mesh panels. They have flat metal rods along each of the long sides to which benches, map frames, waste disposal baskets and so on can be attached. The mesh

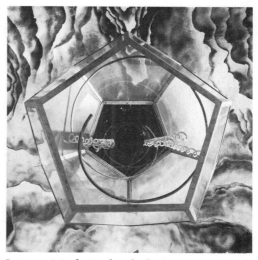

Lennart Mörk: Dodecahedron incorporating the black hole of the universe, Tekniska Högskolan station.

Åke Pallarp: Sign indicating the Stadion exit at the station of that name.

is covered with a layer of electrostatically sprayed epoxy to give a soft, lattice-like impression as well as making the surface difficult to damage. The panels afford protection against walls which may become wet. The plastic covering makes it possible to use a variety of colours, which helps to distinguish between stations.

In the Masmo pedestrian tunnel and in the linking tunnels and end parts of the Stadion and Tekniska Högskolan stations, the metal mesh was removed from walls so that the concrete-sprayed rock face itself could give the stations their characteristic landmarks and break the monotony. This is where the artists concentrated their efforts, and besides making the areas more attractive and more expressive, it made it easier to recognize the stations and gave them greater individuality.

The first two stations on the Täby line, Stadion and Tekniska Högskolan, were the breakthrough for cave stations. They soon attracted an enormous amount of praise, and were awarded the Kasper Salin prize of the Swedish Architects' Society for 1973. The jury justified the award as follows:

"A good collective transport environment is of great importance for very many people in the city. The two underground stations are examples of simple, uncluttered and stimulating environment achieved by the successful combination of functional and technical requirements on the one hand, and innovative artistic imagination and expression on the other. They demonstrate the important part played by artistic expression in our physical environment, and indicate its potential; in so doing, they serve as models for future developments in our collective environment."

Precise roles to be played by the *dramatis personae* became more clearly defined after the trial of strength at Stadion and Tekniska Högskolan. All artists could now take an active part even at the planning stage. Thanks to the interest in artistic questions, flexibility and diplomatic talents of Michael Granit, the architect in charge, it was possible to fend off a threat to hand over total control to contractors. When new stations were added to lines 2 and 3, the metal mesh panels were taken away. On line 3 (the Järva line), the

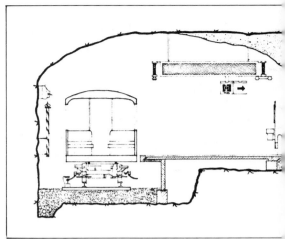

Ulrik Samuelson and Per H Reimers: Sketch for a wall of the connecting passage with "Waterfall", at Kungsträdgården station.

Drainage of "natural" water at platform level.

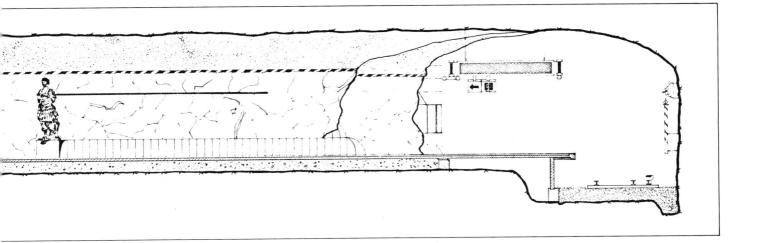

"Waterfall", with water fed partly from natural sources.

Joining of two floor patterns without alignment.

Ulrik Samuelson: The eastern exit at Kungsträdgården station.

Demonstration model for Kungsträdgården station.

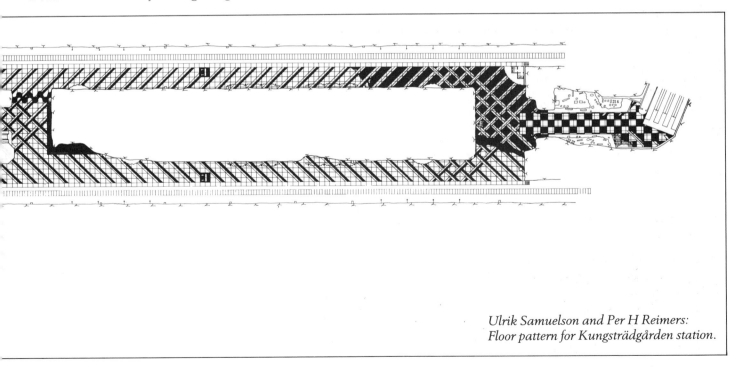

Ulrik Samuelson and Per H Reimers:
Floor pattern for Kungsträdgården station.

ceiling was turned into a baffle construction serving the same purpose as the standard for line 2, but more open, so that the rock arch covered in sprayed concrete was visible between the baffles. The layer of sprayed concrete was made thicker and the drainage behind it improved, so that salt deposits and leakages were further reduced.

One of the last of the 1970s stations, Kungsträdgården, which is centrally located close to big cultural institutions, important places and buildings in Stockholm, and underneath the Kungsträdgården park itself, gave rise to thoughts about an underground garden – the Swedish name translates as "King's Garden". For the first time, the bare rock face was exposed all the way along the platform walls: experience and the fact that people had got used to cave stations made this "risk" permissible. Channeling away the water both from its source and from the floor involved a lot of technical difficulties. The park, the location, the cultural institutions and the rock combined to form a theme on which the artist Ulrik Samuelson proceeded to play variations in masterly fashion. In no other station has the contribution made by artists had such widespread influence as in Kungsträdgården station, where the overall artistic vision even extends to affect the neutral area outside the station entrance, and can be detected in virtually every detail.

New and cheaper blasting techniques have resulted in the fact that all stations on the Täby and Järva lines are at a depth of some 20 to 30 metres, apart from the ones at Kista, which is a surface station on a viaduct, and at Danderyds Sjukhus, which is a concrete station directly below the surface.

Good visibility was regarded as an important requirement, and as a result, wherever possible, ticket halls do not have pillars, and lifts and shafts are open to view. Inclined lifts are linked openly with escalators, and are virtually miniature mountain railways.

Untreated concrete has generally been used for walls in the ticket halls, cast against rippled boards or smooth moulds; rough cast and terrazzo have also been used. The colour of stations, decided in consultation with the artists concerned, recurs in the ticket halls, pedestrian tunnels and stairways. Extra colour is provided by adver-

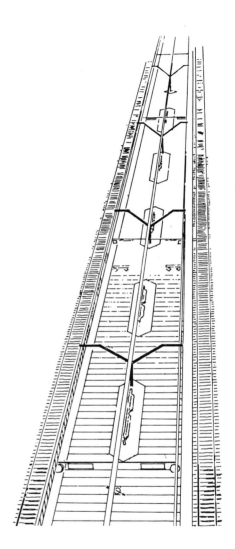

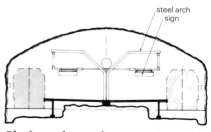

Platform plan and cross-sections of the trumpet stations on the Södra Järva line.

tisements, kiosks and shops. Ceilings are basically of the platform type, made of metal mesh units in aluminium. Street exits have been designed so as to be immediately recognizable as part of the underground, with common design characteristics and the "T" emblem as a logo for the whole network.

The new type of structural components used during the 1970s mean that building time is greatly reduced, and they do not obstruct traffic in the track tunnels.

Reductions in cost amounting to about 10% per station, that is roughly 1 million kronor at 1973 price levels, as a result of the new station design meant that more money was available to pay artists for their efforts. However, not all the savings, which could have been used for such things as more durable and expensive materials, have been taken advantage of.

Characteristic of the very latest cave stations bringing the new building programme of the 1980s to completion are bare rock surfaces, larger spans and an improved range of visibility. The baffle ceilings have been opened up and redesigned as lengthwise baffles only with a span of 36 m suspended from frame structures, over the platform area, within a single impressive and continuous arch.

Common to all extensions of the underground network is the fact that all the stations have been designed by eminent architects, even if the construction side has been the responsibility of engineers and builders. Despite variations in aims and attitudes, each decade has produced stations of lasting architectural value. Unfortunately, the overall architectural pattern has seldom been left intact by subsequent developments. Changes in advertising fashions, for instance, have meant that the placing and design of hoardings at many stations have ruined the architectural details of the walls alongside the tracks. The closing down of news-stands and shops on the platforms and in ticket halls has also left behind more or less unhealed wounds in the overall station enviroment. Nevertheless, it is clear that the Stockholm underground stations, and especially the new cave stations, are generally appreciated by the regular passengers for whom they were built.

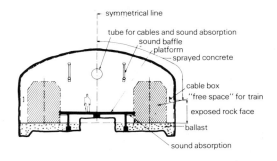

symmetrical line
tube for cables and sound absorption
sound baffle
platform
sprayed concrete
cable box
"free space" for train
exposed rock face
ballast
sound absorption

Prelude

MAILIS STENSMAN

Just imagine it! Every morning at about 7 o'clock, then again every afternoon, going down into a black hole! It's a bit on the cold and damp side down there, some 30 metres below ground. What could be done to make it, if not exactly enjoyable then at least tolerable, descending into these underground labyrinths twice a day on the way to and from work? Not to feel the pressure of 30 metres of primeval rock over our heads, but instead to find the underground caverns a rather pleasant experience, something to set our imagination going, poetic perhaps, or just a little bit provocative.

That's what it can be like, if artists take their job seriously and work together with the authorities, engineers and architects to create a total environment. And that is what has happened over the years, more and more successfully, in the Stockholm underground. You can see the chronological development, and if only people had listened sooner to the ideas put forward by artists and others concerned at an early stage, the whole process of creating an artistically inspired environment would have been quicker.

When I read what was written in the 1940s, in order to get some idea of the background to the project of sending art underground, the beginnings of what has now blossomed forth into something unique in the history of Swedish art, I can feel the joy and expectations people experienced at the very thought. It's as if they could already see before their very eyes the Järva line of the 1970s with its string of stations, each one a glistening pearl. You can read these enthusiastic articles in the 1949 issues of *Konst och Kultur* (Art and Culture) and *Tidskrift för föreningen Konst åt folket*. (The "Art for the People" Society Journal). It was the artists, and above all the concretists, who saw even then what architects, engineers and artists could do if they cooperated to work the miracle. If only there had been a realistic platform for their cooperation, the work would have been in full swing by then, at the end of the forties and in the early fifties! But the authority concerned, Stockholm Tramways, were not interested in allowing artists to use their expertise and create stimulating environments in these caverns that were being built for humans to pass through. In fact, their attitude was one of distrust and scepticism. According to the plans, advertisements were to provide the only form of artistic expression allowed down there. The situation at that time was such that politicians could not see the point of measures to let art play a natural role in public buildings.

How did people at the end of the 1940s think the underground and its collective transport system could be made pleasant? How was art to gain an accepted place in everyday environments? How could the old thirties slogan—"Art for the People"—be made a reality? The editor and cultural journalist Per Olov Zennström sent round a questionnaire and printed the results in *Konst och Kultur* under the heading: "Abstract Art or Adverts for 'Canned Gruel'?": many interesting suggestions were received. An even earlier seed in this discussion was sown by Stellan Mörner, a member of the Halmstad Group, in an article entitled "Art in Waiting Rooms", published in *Konst och Kultur* 5/1946. He wrote among other things: "It seems to me that in general, towns have far too much art whereas rural districts have nothing at all . . . I saw so many deadly dull places in Småland as recently as last summer. Young people wander about full of hope, waiting and waiting . . . Is not every contribution towards overcoming this feeling of being overlooked, of living in a forgotten environment, a communal duty? I believe a work of art could brighten up the atmosphere and stimulate people, give rise to discussion and admiration, and become a topic of conversation. And waiting rooms are a natural location where people come together." Stellan Mörner concluded his plea with the words: "And then one hears there is money available to make station buildings more attractive" referring no doubt to *Statens Konstråd* (the Swedish Art Advisory Council), which was founded in 1937 with the task of supplying public buildings with art.

However, in keeping with the traditional way of looking at things, it was mainly a different type of building that was supplied with works of art by the Art Council—despite the fact that Arthur Engberg, who would nowadays be called the Minister of Education, expressed himself enthusiastically thus in an official report: "The time is already long past when an interest in art was considered to be

Lennart Rodhe: Vignette, 1949.

the privilege of a few. Nowdays, both interest in and understanding of art is growing apace. Art is well on the way to being everybody's property. In public buildings, assembly halls, workplaces, factories and offices, the presence of works of art has become more and more appreciated. We must do all we can to encourage this development.'' (SOU 1936:50.)

But back to *Konst och Kultur* 3/1949, with its cover designed by Lage Lindell and an introductory illustration intended as a challenge, by Lennart Rodhe, who was at that time busy with his wall for the General Post Office in Östersund, ''Endless Parcels''. Under the heading ''Art Goes Underground'', Per Olov Zennström introduced replies to his questionnaire as follows:

" The generation of Swedish artists that has emerged after the Second World War has been discussing the limitations of their traditional activities. They don't just want to paint pictures for hanging in drawing rooms and exhibition galleries. They want whole walls and whole rooms. And of course, it would be unreasonable to expect artists to be satisfied for ever and ever with the kind of painting that came with the Renaissance—when paintings were removed from church walls and hung in private mansions. There is an increasing demand nowadays for art to return to public places and large public buildings, and creating such art naturally presents new problems and demands new forms. **"**

There follow about 20 replies from architects, artists, local officials and future underground passengers. The first is by Erik Ahlsén who, together with his brother Tore Ahlsén, an architect, had been working on a project to liven up façades in Årsta centre in the early 1940s:

" It would be nice if there could be cooperation between architects and builders on the one hand and artists on the other, even while the underground is actually being constructed. Our industrialized age leads to standardization and uniformity, and to cultural impoverishment, unless we all make every effort to introduce variation and cultural richness into the human environment. „

Olle Bonniér continues:

“ What I myself would find the most appropriate way of going about things is not to commission paintings for this purpose, not to allow some individual painters or other to bask in solitary splendour, but instead to look for a collective solution.

The ideal which would be not only the fairest but also the most successful way of proceeding would be to select two groups of artists who could combine to tackle the job collectively. One group of older painters (i e naturalists) and one group of younger ones (concretists), with about three or four in each. „

“ Art for the people, doing one's bit to bring about just a small portion of the enormous tasks involved in the programme. Let us hope we are spared an avalanche of adverts and posters in the new underground. The ideal would be for architects, painters and sculptors to come together at an early stage and sort out the decorative side. It would also be a good idea to try out various ways of achieving the aims, so that we can be sure of using the best method in future—after all, this is only the beginning of the underground. „
(Jerker Eriksson, artist)

“ . . . paint the various stations in different colours, so that they are recognizable as the red one or the blue one—if you like, decorate them with stripes and spots! The main thing is, they must be fun places. I've never seen anything more miserable than the mousey grey rubbish adorning present underground stations. No, get rid of uniformity! Incidentally, giving the stations their own colour would be going back to an old Stockholm tradition, although it was the various surface railway lines that had different colours in the old days—the red line, the yellow line, and the blue.

In any case, the main thing is that there should be a bit of colour down there. „
(Sven Erixson, ''X-et'')

Vera Nilsson and the mosaic specialist Toni Piovesana with their pillar at T-Centralen, 1957.

" Large areas should be in various striking colours with ornamentation where necessary, purely for its own sake or as a contrast to the empty spaces. Artists should work together with architects on the walls. I want no advertising, I want art designed for tunnels—unashamedly abstract. "
(Randi Fisher)

" Obviously, artists should look after the walls, but not in a haphazard way—there must be a point behind it all. In other words, a well-designed composition, where people are not onlookers but partakers. A symphony of movement, circulation, colour and form, full of rhythm. For instance, a passage or a corridor must not be filled with static pictures, interesting reliefs and posters advertising gruel: that would merely make people stop and look, wear out the individual and cause collisions as people stream by. On the other hand, some continuous, rhythmical ornamentation, for instance, would help the stream to flow. Stations, however, should be designed bearing in mind that they are places where passengers break off their journey, pause a while, then move on again. They should perhaps have heavier forms, calmer colours, horizontal and vertical lines, etc.

I thus think the whole thing should be abstract. So: no unmotivated motifs, but instead motivated colours and shapes with an aesthetic function (and why not a practical one as well). It has to be a pleasure to take an underground ride. "
(Arne Jones)

" Obviously, one can argue about whether painters and sculptors should be involved in the underground at all—but in my view, they should. However, in that case there must be cooperation between artists, architects and engineers at as early a stage as possible.

It isn't just a matter of hanging pictures or setting up sculptures if you are going to decorate an underground. I think the main thing is the ambience itself, giving stations, halls and passages a bright and cheerful character. A breath of fresh air is needed in the underground, and not just through the ventilators!

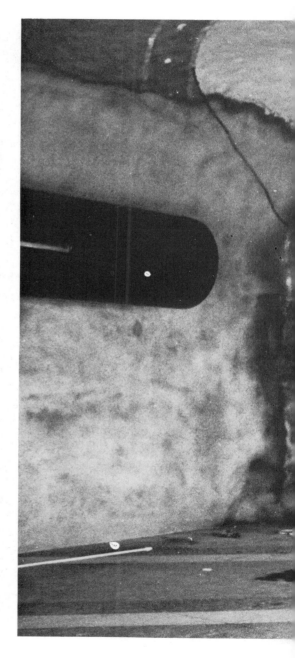

Ulrik Samuelson painting Kungsträdgården station.

It isn't just the walls that need working on. I think you can do quite a lot with things like bannisters and signs. A playful touch wouldn't do any harm. It would be fun, for instance, to decorate the tunnel into which the trains disappear in an amusing way.

If people really do want architects, engineers and artists to work together and solve the problems posed by the new underground, then I think painters and sculptors are ready for such cooperation right now. 𝅘

(Lage Lindell)

❝ Nowdays stations are the natural meeting place for crowds of people, and should therefore be the obvious place for artistic treatment on a grand scale. Architects, engineers and artists ought to be working together at an early stage.

Colours and shapes can be used in such a way that they help to direct passengers and make it easier for them to move around. The creation of works of art and practical building work should go hand in hand. The coming and going of trains, everything should be a part of an image planned in advance to work in all sorts of ways.

Let us avoid making the place feel like a cellar, and instead make every station a composition, a jewel in the crown for the city. This would give stopping places a character of their own and make travelling on the underground a pleasant and varied experience. 𝅘

(Pierre Olofsson)

❝ I think it's about time the West tried to create a bit of culture and took a few new initiatives instead of just wasting time and paper on talk about defending old cultural values. One such move would be to make the new underground into a refreshing oasis instead of a mousehole one is forced to go down into in order to get to work. Make the underground a haven where you can take refuge from the rat-race for a while! 𝅘

(Uno Vallman)

Jörgen Fogelquist at work on Västertorp station, January 1982.

Helga Henschen and her assistant at Tensta station, 1975.

" I am very sceptical about fixed decorations in general. A wall covered with colourful posters is surely just as good, and it would be odd if Swedish posters could not be made as artistically attractive as those of Switzerland and Denmark, for instance.

Actually, I also think we should have more adverts in the town itself, good adverts. Think what a bright and lively impression the town would make if we could put a little colour onto all those empty gable ends and building sites. "
(Eskil Almgren, Commissioner, Buildings Department)

" Why shouldn't artists help architects to create an environment down there in the underground which doesn't make us feel too depressed? No doubt it would be better for cooperation to take place between architects and artists, so that everybody doesn't suffer as a result. "
(Holger Blom, gardener, Municipal Parks Department)

" What should we do, then? I think myself that artistic imagination and creativity should be given free rein and encouraged to make suggestions. Of course we can have monumental paintings and sculptures as well as artistic architectural creations. The idea behind the decorating of the Moscow underground stations seems to me to be a good one, namely, that each station is given a particular theme. One of them, for instance, is decorated exclusively with marble from the Urals, another is dedicated to the heroes in the war against Nazism, a third is a hymn in praise of work in its various forms. "
(Knut Olsson, Deputy Vice Chairman of the Stockholm City Council)

" We don't have in this country a firmly based decorative tradition like they have in Norway, of which Oslo's new town hall is a good example. But we do have the potential over here as well, and he who dares wins! "
(Olof Hansson, student)

" If you have to wait for a long time between trains, you'll be able to become an art expert! My God, just think how many people will rush to ride on the underground if this business actually comes to anything! "
(Carola Mattsson, laundry worker)

" Art is always enjoyable, and to have art at work would be really something! I think artistically designed posters wouldn't be out of place, either. Preferably funny ones, so that there's something to laugh at. I know they have some very funny posters in London, but here they're just as goddammed boring as the new housing estates. But like I said, bright and pleasant places with lots of art, such as reliefs with Stockholm themes or work motifs, that would be the kind of thing future underground passengers will want. "
(Martin Gustafsson, tram driver)

Obviously, there was plenty of enthusiasm and optimism about the opportunity of getting to grips with these underground caverns destined to be used by so many people. Several of the comments, by both artists and architects, insist that cooperation at an early stage is of crucial importance if the project is to succeed. The subterranean stations must have been seen as stimulating challenges, with all their hustle and bustle. They were completely new and different environments to work with. They were everyday places but without the awkward atmosphere of formality, power, breeding . . . or what ever functions they were that houses up on the surface were supposed to be burdened with. Exhilaration and a bold lack of respect cry out from the written suggestions, and they are miles away from the pretentious, at times rather boring, careful and routine works of art created both then and now in our more or less public buildings of various kinds.

It is above all the concretists, "the men of 1947" led by Olle Bonniér, Pierre Olofson and Lennart Rodhe, whose proposals were an attempt to overcome the isolation of art and lead it out into the everyday life of society.

What was the reaction of KRO, Konstnärernas Riksorganisation (the National Organization of Artists), to these discussions, when these ideas, the most forward-looking ones of the 1940s, were expressed? Were they perhaps fully occupied by the growing market for easel art designed for more or less private consumption?

The concretists' ideas, which didn't even get as far as the sketch stage, were discussed further in talks with the chief architect for the underground, Gunnar Lené. In broad outline they involved stressing a vertical axis so that characteristic features above ground should be continued down into the subterranean stations. Underneath Konserthuset, the Concert Hall, which had been painted sky-blue in the 1920s, the idea was that Hötorget station should also have blue as its dominant colour, while Rådmansgatan station should reflect the golden colour of the City Library, Stadsbiblioteket, and so on. The horizontal axis should be carried through by giving coaches on the different lines characteristic colours: one line should be red, another blue or yellow.

"It turned out to be a damp squib. We had a dream. We thought there would be lots of stations," says Pierre Olofsson, who was elected to represent the concretist group.

A big meeting was held at the Sports Palace, and all the brilliant, effervescent ideas collapsed like a house of cards.

"Nobody came, apart from the advertising boys. I was shattered. We asked for money so that we could work on our ideas and present them in more detail in sketch form so that they could see how to go about it. We wanted money, and advertising boys were supposed to give money. Absolute silence. Then I got mad. End of cooperation. But we cast bread on the waters. Everybody thought the ideas were good. The colour business was adopted, even if it was only tiles all the same colour. What we envisaged was art, something stirring. It was to be a total vision."

Much later, in the 1970s, the Rådhuset station on the Järva line has tiles the same colour as Carl Westman's Rådhus (Town Hall) up above it, and the effect is completed by references to the history of the Kungsholmen district in which it stands. Even Lage Lindell's idea that "it would be fun to decorate the tunnel into which the trains disappear in an amusing way" is realized in that station, designed by Sigvard Olsson.

Pierre Olofsson ended our interview (in February 1985) with a sigh: "We were young. There was opposition from the older artists in KRO. Eventually they had a competition and chose a hotch-potch. T-Centralen was a dog's dinner."

Concrete stations with walls covered in pale-coloured tiles, like public lavatories, continued to be built. The images that were allowed to break the monotony were the pictures and mating calls of advertisements. Strong voices still maintained that there should be nothing but advertisements in the underground. Many people had obviously been captivated by the moulded white tiles of the Paris metro stations, the yellow tiled patterns like gilded frames round enormous advertising posters, and most of all by the mass of adverts. Even the occasional artist, getting on in years, talked lyrically about advertising posters and the Paris atmosphere. As if Stockholm could breath Parisian air by sticking up advertising posters in the underground and all over the town!

It is understandable that the battle for this underground territory was hard. In 1945 a delegation from Stockholm visited the Moscow underground. The stations there had been made into new palaces for the people, and had no advertising at all. An underground without adverts was not considered good, neither on financial grounds nor from the point of view of what an underground system in a large city ought to look like. The powers that argued for nothing but adverts were strong, and still are. Advertising produces a steady and not insignificant source of revenue for the owners.

The prize building project of the postwar period, this subterranean transport machine, would gulp down masses of people day after day, year after year, into its excavated or blasted passages and chambers, and also into its surface stations in the Stockholm suburbs. Today, it is calculated that 50 million people pass through T-Centralen every year. It is natural that these centres of passage and waiting should be attractive to the persuasive slogan-makers and

Aston Forsberg and Birger Forsberg: Relief for Slussen station.

advertisers. There is money to be made out of firms who buy advertising space, and by those who sell it.

Many Swedish artists, among them the concretists, had made study trips to Norway at the end of the forties and beginning of the fifties, mainly to Oslo where they could study the Norweigan monumental painting which had been gathering strength for several decades, created by artists like Per Krogh, Axel Revold, Alf Rolfsen, Aage Storstein and others. In 1950, the Oslo Town Hall was inaugurated, filled with frescos, reliefs and sculptures by many artists. There and in some earlier achievements, such as Edvard Munch's frescos and paintings at the Freia chocolate works in Oslo, artists had played a very prominent role. Almost every wall in the Town Hall was covered completely by paintings depicting Norwegian history. It demonstrated a fantastic method of working with images. It may be that one did not always appreciate the style, which was frequently heroic or tinged with cubism; but the fact that art had been allowed to play such an important role inspired thoughts on how images might be used even in our more cautious climate. Inspiring traces of Mexican murals, also passed on by Western intermediaries, gave rise to more ideas about how walls can talk.

The Danish painter, Georg Jacobsen, who had worked together with the up-and-coming Mexican mural painter Diego Rivera, was Professor at the Oslo Art Academy in the late thirties. Theoretical formal problems had interested Jacobsen and Rivera when they were analysing older war-paintings from the Renaissance onwards. Both of them returned home and proceeded to create murals.

The battle to send art underground continued during the first half of the 1950s. Klara station, or T-Centralen as it is now called, began to near completion. It was to be the central point of the network, but as yet no decision had been taken to provide it with works of art. The two admirably stubborn artists Vera Nilsson and Siri Derkert reacted in different ways, Siri in more impromptu and agitated fashion, Vera Nilsson more thoughtfully. Letter after letter was sent to Commissioner Hjalmar Mehr, and at the same time politicians in the Clarté movement, where Lage Lindell was also active, were won over to support the idea of art underground, among them John Takman.

Vera Nilsson wrote to Hjalmar Mehr:

"It's about the underground. We want fun, cheerfulness and a blaze of colour in the underground. This is the motorway used every day by ordinary people, those without cars . . . In the old days people had churches, and they were inundated with everything the country had to offer in the way of art. They were filled with unimaginable treasures . . . Let us create similar places under the earth, underground cathedrals! Every stopping place a fairytale palace! . . . Bear in mind that Sweden has a whole army of magicians who could make that dream come true! . . . I enclose an issue of *Konst och Kultur* from 1949, in which the topic is debated . . . Call in the artists! It's high time . . . May I also ask for an appointment so that we can discuss these matters further."

Hjalmar Mehr replied quickly in a letter dated 26 March: " . . . I am most interested in the question. I have taken certain measures to prepare myself and find out more about it, and I would be pleased to meet you and discuss it in more detail."

Gradually, the tone of the letter became more personal: "If, by pooling our resources once again, we have achieved something for the people, we can be pleased with ourselves. In the hope that together we shall be able to strike more blows in the cause of justice, freedom, truth, art . . ." The upper level of T-Centralen was a reality.

John Takman was also being active from his quarter, the Communist Party, and had got in first with a motion placed before the Stockholm Municipal Council. On 18 April, 1955, it was signed as motion No 24 by John Takman and Karin Nordlander. Shortly afterwards came motion No 25 from the Social Democrats, signed by Stellan Arvidson, Sten Andersson, Wilhelm Forsberg, Inga Thorsson and others. Wilhelm Forsberg was later to take an active part in the work of Trafikens konstnämnd—the Stockholm Transport Art Advisory Council—when the Greater Stockholm Council took over responsibility for the underground.

The first of these motions reads as follows:

Vera Nilsson: "The Klara which will live on, in spite of everything". Pillar at T-Centralen, 1957.

"In the opinion of the undersigned it is regrettable that the latter points (i e that art experts should be consulted at an early stage) have thus far been ignored. All the underground stations currently in operation are adorned, or rather disfigured, with commercial posters . . . The underground has become a new and much appreciated part of Stockholm's profile, a meeting place and a feature used by the majority of the city's population. We cannot remain indifferent to the image presented by the underground, the most frequently used facility in the whole capital, to both transport personnel and passengers. We consider it to be extremely urgent for the central stations to be designed differently from those opened so far, and that the design of the latter should also be reexamined. In our view it is feasible to give every station an identity: one could have frescos while another could have mosaics, for instance. We therefore propose that the City Council request the appropriate authority to rapidly set up a working party to report on the artistic decoration of underground stations."

The other motion, No 25 from the Social Democrats, says among other things:

"Perhaps not every underground station can be turned into a fairytale palace. Nevertheless, painters and sculptors, ceramists and craftsmen should work together with architects and engineers, and be given the opportunity to turn the underground stations into attractive places and stimulating environments, and also to transform a few of the main stations into underground cathedrals, fanfares of colour and rhythm . . . We therefore propose that the City Council should take action to ensure the underground stations achieve a higher level of aesthetic quality, and that as a first step, a competition be organized to endow the forthcoming station in Klara with good art."

We can recognize quotations from Vera Nilsson's letter to Hjalmar Mehr, and also viewpoints from the discussion in *Konst och Kultur*.

The T-Centralen competition

And so a start was made on what was eventually to become a political decision to advertise the first competition. Motions were referred to the Tramways Company, the Highways Commission, and the Council for the Protection of the Cultural and Natural Values of the City of Stockholm (Stockholms skönhetsråd). Naturally enough, the latter body supported the motion, but recommended that efforts be concentrated on the larger stations particularly suitable for decorative treatment, suggesting that in the first place there should be a competition for the Klara station (i e T-Centralen). Stockholm Tramways Ltd responded by stating their pleasure at the interest shown by the proposers in artistic embellishment of the underground stations. They pointed out, however, that from the very start of the project great care had been taken with the architectural design, even though the primary aim was to satisfy functional requirements. They defended themselves against accusations that advertising had had a disfiguring effect: "Since lively and colourful posters, preferably produced with artistic advice, are, in the opinion of the company, in keeping with the nature of the underground as a main traffic artery, advertising has been allowed wherever possible."

The Highways Commission, like the two other bodies, recommended a competition, but joined the Tramways Company in suggesting it should include the Gamla Stan and Slussen stations as well as T-Centralen. They also expressed their approval of the underground extension already completed: "The architectural design was handled within the company by qualified architects very familiar with the relevant questions of design and colour. It is the view of the Highways Commission that the stations completed so far are examples of good architecture, well suited to their function and to the technical and financial restrictions imposed."

Although the Moscow underground was not specifically mentioned in the motions, both the Tramways Company and the Highways Commission felt compelled to mention it as a comparison. The tramways report pointed out that the Moscow underground had greater freedom, since it is so deep that there was no need to

81

worry about the financial consequenses of entry in connection with its generously sized and richly decorated stations. The Highways Commission questioned the artistic quality of the Moscow stations. "The underground stations built in Moscow during the last ten years are often maintained to be exemplary. Not everyone shares this opinion, however. Many people feel the Moscow stations are a pompous display of undesirable pastiche in mixed historical styles, originating in buildings quite different in kind from underground stations." After stating their functionalist credo, however, they are nevertheless in favour of a significant contribution by artists to the stations not yet built: "Such cooperation, however, should not be limited to the occasional wall surface being handed over to the artists for treatment. Such isolated bits of wall would risk giving the impression of being aesthetically out of place in their context. The whole area must be regarded as an entity, and artists should therefore cooperate with architects and use suitable materials for floor, wall and roof so as to create a harmonious artistic whole suited to the function of a station. Practical details, such as barriers, newsstands, signs and so on should be treated as integral parts of the whole." Little of this integrated approach was in evidence, however, in the first of the "decorated" stations, even though the contest included many individual items and fittings as possible areas of competition.

The Commissioners' Council and the Central Board of Administration accepted the recommendations received, and proposed a competition aimed at achieving a higher quality of decoration in at least the centrally situated stations, to be carried out by artists in consultation with architects. The Tramways Company was requested to organize a prize competition, and representatives of the Central Board of Administration and the Highways Commission should be included on the prize committee. The proposal was duly accepted by the City Council.

The debate in the City Council made it clear who had formulated the proposal from the Commissioners' Council, and it was not the Highways Commissioner, whose job it actually was to speak to it.

The first to speak was Social Commissioner Hjalmar Mehr, who was neither the official presenter of the proposal nor the chairman of the Commissioners. As related in the previous chapter, Vera Nilsson had been working very hard to ensure that art was given a role in the underground, and in that connection had visited the chief architect of the Tramways Company, Magnus Ahlgren, together with Liss Eriksson and Lage Lindell. Ahlgren advised her to turn to Mehr. According to what she told Liss Eriksson she had enjoyed an enthusiastic reception even on her second visit: he told her that money was available, and he was sure the aim could be achieved. Mehr's enthusiasm was reflected in his speech to the City Council which, as was so often the case in matters that interested him, was forceful, eloquent and long. He said among other things:

"No doubt everyone has heard that a Parisian spends four years of his life in the underground. The fact that people have to spend so much time travelling to and from work is quite simply one of the curses of modern civilization. One could hold forth about the tragedy of long distances in modern society.

When you look at it in this light, it is of no small significance that such important places should be as bright, as attractive and as easy to negotiate as possible. Anyone who travels on the underground should not have to feel oppressed by the sensation of being in a tunnel, or shut inside a barrel, as you might say. While people are in underground stations, they ought not to have that oppressive feeling of being down under the ground. It's quite another matter when you are in a bus or a tram and can look out of the window at the countryside. —

That is why it is quite natural and reasonable to pay a lot of attention to the artistic design of underground stations, and on behalf of the group and also for myself, I would like to say how pleased I am that we all thought exactly the same. How important it is that something really has to be done is underlined by the board's proposal—that the prize committee which will judge the entries should consist of delegates representing the Central Board of Administration, the Highways Commission and the Tramways

Board. This is not a problem for a particular authority to decide, but to the highest degree one for the whole town, for all citizens, and hence it is a problem which must be solved by the City Council.

I would suggest that it is now extremely urgent for all those concerned with this question to get down to work as efficiently as possible. No time must be lost. We must not find there is no time to conduct the competition for administrative reasons, or that the underground stations are finished before the winners can make their contributions. —

I know from visits and personal contacts that the artists themselves are extremely interested. The question has already been discussed in their journals, and you could say that some of the preliminary work has already been done. What must happen now is that artists, architects and tramway engineers must cooperate in such a way that everything goes quickly and smoothly, so that it is possible for us to obtain some idea of just what this kind of artistic decoration is going to look like.''

One of the subsequent speakers was the Financial Commissioner Erik Huss, who stressed how urgent the matter really was: the Highways Commission had been sitting on the proposal for several months, and time was now getting very short. In his formal capacity as a deputy member of the Tramways Board, he had already discussed the matter with their management and could inform the council that the very next day they would contact the KRO, the National Organization of Artists, and that a week later the board would have before it proposals as to what form the competition should take and how it should be set in motion. It was imperative for the board to act as speedily as this, since as he had made clear, they only had a few months to complete the whole business.

Only nine days later, on 28th March, 1956, the competition was in fact announced. Time really was short: construction of the future T-Centralen station was already far advanced.

The big public competition was conducted under severe time pressure. Less than two months were allowed for sketches. Klara station, to be renamed T-Centralen, was already under construc-

Kungsträdgården →

↗ Rullband från T-centralen

tion. There was no time to lose if there was to be any art in there at all. By the closing date, no less than 156 entries had been received.

It was interesting to note that the competition invited four different types of proposals: 1) design for the two separate ticket halls, of which the western one closest to the Central Railway Station should be completely devoid of advertising, 2) the upper platform area walls, roof, floor and pillars, or ideas for one or possibly half a long wall in this area, which was also to be free from advertising, suggestions for colours and the treatment of pillars, floor and roof and certain fittings in the lower platform area, which was to have a normal amount of advertising, 3) the connecting passage between the underground and the Central Railway Station, and 4) specific details such as the floor alone, bannisters, certain sculptural features, etc. The second category was looking for an overall integrated design for the station area. But with only two months in which to make sketches, proposing overall designs in what was such a new, untried, large and complicated location must be regarded as impossible. It must be said that a positive point in the programme was the clear statement that "in this hall there will be no posters or other form of advertising, but the hall will be reserved exclusively for artistic decoration." The programme singles out the roof for artistic treatment, and mentions the possibility of doing something artistic with the floor on three occasions. It was not until much later in the history of the underground that people could enter an area designed as an integrated whole, enter into a work of art, and find images all around them, in the roof, on the floor, and on the walls.

In accordance with the council recommendations (formally, of course, the competition was organized by the board of the Tramways Company), the jury included several prominent local counsellors. In practice, however, the influence of the politicians was slight: actual judging took place during one week in May, 1956, and was conducted by the artist members nominated by the National Organization of Artists—Sven Erixson (X:et), Olle Gill, Tor Hörlin, Bror Marklund, Karl Axel Pehrson, Sven Sahlberg and Liss Eriksson.

The recommendations of the artist members for prizes, and the reasons for the awards, were accepted by the rest of the prize committee. Part of it reads as follows:

"The unusual nature of the tasks set and the large number of entries has made judging difficult. Many of the entries display a wealth of ideas, expressiveness, and a high level of artistic quality: the prize committee would like to state that in its view, the competition has been a great success. However, no entry has provided an integrated solution to the problems set. The jury believes this can be achieved by combining and in some cases adjusting various proposals. By a unanimous decision, the jury has decided to award prizes to 27 entries, of which it is recommended that 16 be put into practice."

The jury's recommendation that 16 of the entries should be put into practice was no guarantee of that actually happening: the final decision was up to the Tramways Company. At the final meeting of the jury, Hjalmar Mehr suggested privately to Liss Eriksson that the artists should make sure they appointed a strong personality to keep an eye on what happened next. Liss Eriksson's formal proposal ensured that a representative of the artists was in fact appointed. Although he was not one hundred percent in favour of plans to bring art into the underground, X:et was their first choice as "strong man"; he felt he was too busy, and so Tor Hörlin and Bror Marklund were selected to assist him, with Karl Axel Pehrson as deputy. They became an advisory body on artistic questions to the Tramways Company, and were to continue in that capacity for almost ten years. Tor Hörlin in particular was often consulted by the company about art and design.

The basis on which judgements had been made on the competition entries was not really satisfactory, due to the lack of time available for making sketches. Some artists found, to their great indignation, that their proposals were rejected after further scrutiny of the winning entries by the architect and the panel of artists. A provisional costing was worked out for each proposal and compared with the so-called normal cost (usually standardized ceramic tiles), and the difference was designated the cost of putting the artistic design into practice. Account was also taken of the loss of advertising revenue. Results showed that the effect of introducing art underground would be a considerable increase in costs, and so all proposals recommended by the jury for Slussen and Gamla Stan were dropped.

A whole series of proposals were realized in the upper platform area and the ticket halls at T-Centralen. Works of art varying in type and technique were suddenly jumbled together with no thought of the overall effect, as if someone had a bad conscience and was trying to put right previous omissions.

The urgent need to begin cooperation between artists, architects and engineers at an early stage in order to create a more or less integrated artistic whole, something which had been discussed in the debate preceding the competition and also stated in the report from the Highways Commission, did not actually come about in fact, of course, due to lack of time. All the works of art had to be finished and in place in 1957. It was not possible to create an integrated environment when as many works as possible, both large and small, were to be included. The preliminary work, the sketches, had been done without individual artists knowing what the others were doing, because of the competitive situation. Some voices on the jury had argued that Erland Melanton's glass prisms should be accommodated on both walls alongside the tracks, but even so the final decision was to spread the work among as many artists as possible. In isolation, and without much in the way of protest, the various artists had produced their work in the limited area allocated to them. An advantage of this approach could be that it gives an opportunity to concentrate on the image itself. Twelve artists were commissioned to work on lines 1 and 2 at T-Centralen, and four of them worked in pairs. Today, the motley collection looks almost like an exhibition of full-scale samples of artistic decor, but in the enthusiasm caused by the new opportunities of creating something, it did not seem like that at the time.

Of those who had agitated for art in the underground from the

Siri Derkert: Woman carrying tiles.

very beginning, only Vera Nilsson and Siri Derkert were actually able to carry out their ideas in practice. Independently of each other they experimented and produced a technique which satisfied the need for durability insisted upon by the Tramways Company. Vera Nilsson made her sketch for a pillar in the form of a paper collage, which was then made into a multi-coloured mosaic in natural stone and glass by two Italian craftsmen. Vera Nilsson herself supplied a key to the four sides of the pillar with the title: "The Klara which will live on, in spite of everything."

Siri Derkert's pillar, her first public work, is the result of a very long series of formal and material experiments which paved the way for her late technique with quick, definitive annotations in a foundation which stiffens rapidly. "There was no need to feel paralysed by the concepts of earlier periods, by any tradition about what should be done in order to get it right," she herself wrote in the journal *Cement och Betong* (Cement and Concrete), 1959. Her competition entry was called "Line", but it is better known nowadays as "The Woman Pillar". When Siri Derkert hastily decided to enter the competition with a proposal for a pillar, she had already completed the sketches for another entry called "On the Way". This also won a prize, but was not recommended for putting into practice. Her reason for making another entry was a plasteline tile received from her friend Ninnan Santesson, which had been easy to shape. "In its unassuming, direct contact with the material, the proposed goug-ings on the concrete pillar express the natural sensitivity of the human hand," wrote the prize committee. Siri had to feel her way forward by various means. She had spontaneously hit upon a new technique with the easily moulded plasteline tile, and now was the time to apply it. She went to one of the Craft Institute's concrete workshops in order to refine the technique. Bearing in mind how quickly concrete hardens, the sides of the pillar had to be divided into three sections which were cast separately in a horizontal posi-tion, with darker, coarser concrete at the base and a layer of lighter, finer concrete on top. When the concrete had hardened sufficiently for gouging on—not too wet, or the scratch marks would simply

refill, and not too hard, or it would be too difficult to work—Siri made her images reflecting mainly the ideological struggle of women. Today it is not easy to make out the motifs, since the reliefs are worn out and dusty. The original eggshell-like surface colour the artist achieved has grown much darker with the passage of time. On old photos it is possible to see how the images are formed by shadow effects, as in one of Siri Derkert's early artist paintings.

On one of the long walls, Erland Melanton and Bengt Edenfalk were given the go-ahead for their mosaic in multi-coloured glass prisms entitled "Klaravagnen", a play on the name of the district and the Swedish word for the constellation "The Plough". Glass designer Bengt Edenfalk provided the expertise for designing the modular system of compressed prisms, which were made at the Skruf glass works. The dominant colour of this wall is light blue, and non-figurative shapes run along its 145-metre length like waves on a shore, or the play of colours in the heavens. The pattern is broken at regular intervals by carefully designed signs bearing the word "T-Centralen". This large glass mosaic, which aroused much enthusiasm at the sketch stage, is one of the works of art which have not stood the test of time, neither technically nor artistically. The glass has lost much of its glitter thanks to the fact that the black dust from the brakes has made frequent metre-long cracks all the way along the wall.

Anders Österlin, one of the leading graphic designers of the late fifties, and the ceramist Signe Persson-Melin combined to produce the corresponding wall in the upper platform area. Specially made stoneware tiles in a wide variety of materials, giving a relief effect, have been let into a white background surface of standard clinker. The figures they form are the artists' very own; sometimes they are variations on ancient symbols or traffic lights. As regards colour, Signe Persson-Melin has started out from the glazes she has used most when making her tea-pots, dishes and bowls, while Anders Österlin was mainly responsible for the composition of the figures. From the material and image point of view, this wall has stood the test of time very well, although the white empty spaces left after the

original signs were removed spoil the composition. It feels fresh, and still radiates humour and subtlety besides being spared noticeable vandalization.

Berndt Helleberg created a non-figurative sculpture round a pillar in black cement, which was originally placed on a staircase down to the lower platform area. The pillar continued up through both storeys, and the shapes of the reliefs varied the theme of the staircase. Now, when the pillar has been cut off and the staircase with Per Olof Ultvedt's bannister in ironwork, "Horizontal and Vertical" is no longer there, the pillar looks a little out of place.

On the platform itself are Egon Möller-Nielsen's beautifully shaped seats, sculptures for sitting on. The seats were made of cast stone (a sort of artificial stone) and had inbuilt heating wires. The short sides are gently and invitingly shaped for people sitting on their own, and the long sides, intended for people sitting together, turn to face each other in smooth curves. Since the seats were moved in connection with the rebuilding of T-Centralen, the heating system no longer works, unfortunately: the sculptures have thus lost one dimension.

The ticket hall nearest the Central Railway Station and the passage leading to it were included in the areas given artistic treatment in 1957. The prize committee changed their original recommendation and entrusted the area to Jörgen Fogelquist. He decided to cover the walls in the ticket hall with tiles painted by himself at a ceramics factory in Spain, since the required glazes with the lead content needed for the strong colours were not permitted in Sweden. This is an example of how ceramic tiles can be used in the hands of a colourist. Two quick, concentrated surface planes in yellow, green, red and white span the walls from floor to ceiling on two opposite sides, giving the area a stimulating sense of vibrating energy. A later addition in 1962, which extends along the northern wall towards the Continental Hotel, gives more of an impression of the organic, windswept shapes of nature.

Two proposals were combined and incorporated into the ticket hall leading to Sergels torg and in the lower station area: a pattern

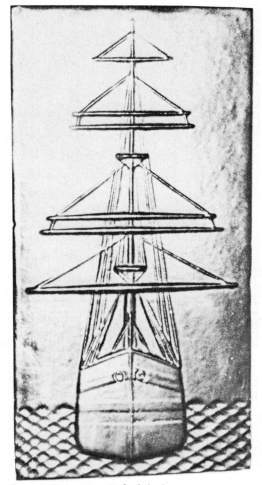

Torsten Treutiger: Relief clinker.

Egon Möller-Nielsen: Sculptured benches at T-Centralen.

composition in Siennese style using different coloured clinkers in black, grey and various shades of white, with a varied relief pattern on implanted clinkers—trams, sailing ships and tram tickets. The pattern was composed by Oscar Brandtberg and the miniature reliefs made by Torsten Treutiger.

In 1958, even before the artistic work on T-Centralen was completely finished, two new motions were put concerning further artistic decorations in the underground network. One of them suggested treatment for the connecting passage between T-Centralen and the Central Railway Station, the other proposed decorative work on the Blackeberg station.

The Tramways Company commented on the motions as follows:

"When decisions were taken concerning decoration at T-Centralen, it was agreed that the connecting tunnel between the T-Centralen station and the Central Railway Station should not receive artistic treatment. The tunnel is currently under construction. Particular attention has been paid to the colour and design of the walls, and advice has been given by the same artists as were responsible for the hall into which the passage leads.

Some 600,000 kronor have been spent on the prize competition, the subsequent discussions and the artistic work on T-Centralen. It would seem advisable to see how people react before deciding to proceed with any more similar decoration. Not everyone agrees about the suitability of art in the underground. Some critics maintain that the underground stations should have nothing more than a carefully composed combination of colours, and possibly a pattern giving each station its particular character. Well-produced advertisements could also serve to reflect the pulsating bustle of passengers and traffic and create an environment in varied colours and styles. The fixed character of the decor would thus be replaced by up-to-the-minute advertising art, on which the artists of today and tomorrow could work.

There can hardly be any question of changing the wall-coverings in any of the relatively recently built stations. On the other hand, more artistic decor might be considered for the (subterranean) stations due to be built for the southwestern line. This is due to open for traffic in 1964.

The prize committee which adjudicated on the artistic decor already put into practice recommended on 31 May, 1956, that a group representing the artists and consisting of Professor S Erixson, artist T Hörlin and sculptor B Marklund, with the artist K A Pehrson as their deputy, should be consulted by the Tramways Company in connection with any future building work which carries out the recommendations made by the prize committee. These artists have kindly made themselves available for discussions on the advertising and certain decorative details at T-Centralen and the Gamla Stan station. It would be appropriate for these artists also to be consulted in connection with any decorative work on future stations.''

The days of von Heland

Hans von Heland, the man in charge of the Tramways Company, was not on the prize committee for the first competition; moreover, the official report from the company in connection with the two 1958 motions had expressed doubt about art in the underground in future. Nevertheless, during the 1960s von Heland came to be so enthusiastic about art in the underground that this period can also be called "the days of von Heland". His interest was so great that some years after his retirement he founded the art gallery Galleri Heland. Many of his colleagues came round to sharing his enthusiasm.

When the motions concerning decoration in the underground came before the Central Board of Administration in April, 1959, reactions were much more positive than those from the Tramways Company had been. Comments had also been received from the Council for the Protection of the Cultural and Natural Values of the City of Stockholm, and from the Highways Commission, both of which supported the setting up of a commission to oversee decoration in the future. The Commissioners' Council, in other words its Chairman Hjalmar Mehr, said among other things:

"Artistic decoration in the T-Centralen station has proved to be a great success from an artistic point of view, and also an element in the overall image of Stockholm which has been much appreciated by passengers and, indeed, by citizens in general. It is thus natural to raise the question of decorating other stations. Financial and artistic interests must be balanced in such a way that a reasonable amount of space at certain stations is reserved for artistic purposes, while at the same time the income received by the Tramways Company from advertising posters is maintained at a high level. It is felt that a decision of the Central Board of Administration, working together with the Tramways Company, should be made concerning the extent of artistic decoration, how many stations should be involved, and which ones, as well as deciding how to go about realizing any such plans. Consultations should take place with representatives of those artists who have worked on the decoration of T-Centralen in the past. A commission of enquiry, which should naturally be given a free hand, should be set up without delay so that artists commissioned to do the work have sufficient time at their disposal."

The outcome of the commission of enquiry was that a new competition was announced for the beginning of December, 1960. Shortly beforehand, as a taste of things to come, one of the prize-winning entries in the 1956 competition had just been realized at Hagsätra: Britta Simonsson's stone mosaic "The Flautists" or "The Melody That Lost Its Way". As early as 1958, moreover, the architects responsible for the Hammarbyhöjden station, had managed to smuggle a little ceramic decoration into the corner of a wall in the ticket hall, a goat by Tom Möller which was actually a materials test using the same kind of tile as was used for the station.

The new competition differed from its predecessor in that more stress was placed on overall solutions. The rock station at Fridhemsplan was to be the model, and regarded as representative of the new stations. Next in line for construction were Östermalmstorg, Mariatorget, Zinkensdamm, Hornstull, Aspudden, and Mälarhöjden. Planned for a later phase were Karlaplan, Gärdet and Ropsten.

Four alternatives were set for the competition: 1) Proposals for decoration without advertisements. 2) Proposals for a mixture of advertising and artistic decoration. 3) Proposals with the main emphasis on advertising about as extensive as in the existing inner-city stations. 4) Proposals for station details, such as floors, bannisters and sculptures. Entries for alternatives 1–3 were expected to cover the choice of materials as well as colour schemes for floors, walls and ceilings.

This time the competition was aimed not only at artists, but also architects, poster designers, etc. As a consequence, the organizations representing architects (SAR), poster designers (SAFFT) and graphic artists (STEFO) asked to be represented on the prize jury.

Prize-money for the competition amounted to 100,000 kronor, which corresponds to well over half a million kronor at 1985 values. Of the 159 entries, 26 were awarded prizes in sections 1 and 4, but only one in section 2. No entry for section 3 was considered worthy of a prize. In its report, the jury stated that there were great difficulties inherent in attempts to combine intensive advertising with posters and meaningful artistic decoration:

"The prize jury has concluded from the results of the competition that the best station environment is achieved when individual stations can be given an overall artistic design, endowing them with a character distinct from that of other stations. This enables the various stations to attain individuality in spite of great technical similarities, and makes it possible for passengers to orientate themselves in a natural way."

The artistic advisory board was very influential when it came to putting the winning entries into practice, with regard both to the individual artist given the job, and which of the stations should receive what art. There was much changing of mind before the prize-winning entries were finally allocated their stations. Siri Derkert's concrete gougings were planned to go into Mariatorget station for a long time, while Karin Björquist's and Kjell Abramson's ceramics were destined for Östermalmstorg—although in fact the latter are now at Mariatorget. For a while it was intended to place Margareta Carlstedt's enamel paintings at Östermalmstorg, but X:et and the rest of the advisory panel thought that station was too central for such a young and little-known artist and so, in 1962, she was replaced by Siri Derkert and asked to create her work of art out at Mälarhöjden. Staffan Hallström's fragmentary ceramic mural now on view at Sergels Torg was long intended for Slussen, together with Sune Fogde's composition in enamel and plaster.

Three weeks before the competition closed, Siri Derkert had found a new concrete material which suited her purpose better than the gouging method which was so difficult to do. The Norwegian Carl Nesjar had specialized in realizing other artists' sketches in blasted concrete, including so-called natural concrete where the motif is formed by dark stone material revealed in the lower layers of what is superficially a flat sheet of marble concrete. Siri experimented by using compressed air to blast out her shapes in a tunnel at Nyboda, was won over completely and became convinced that everybody should start blasting. Since she was 73 years old, however, she was forced to concede that she was unable to blast areas totalling 300 × 3 metres unaided. When it was finally decided where her work would be located, she commissioned assistants to do the blasting on the basis of her sketches in 1964—besides Nesjar she appointed the Kontiki voyager Erik Hesselberg and Valter Janson—and made her sketches full-scale on one of the walls in the enormous tram depot at Eriksbergsplan. Her rather difficult, impressionistic drawings are made up primarily of motifs featuring women and peace. Alongside the platform the concrete changes colour in some places and becomes black, so that the work looks like a photographic negative.

Siri Derkert had lots of ideas about what the station as a whole should look like. The only noticeable traces of these ideas are small areas of untreated rock on the short sides of the platform. The marble concrete was an excellent surface for scribbling on, and as the years passed by the defacing became increasingly dense, as happened in the New York subway trains. After a lively debate, in the course of which Siri's son Carlo Derkert defended the "graffiti", the walls were eventually cleaned at enormous cost and coated with a protective film which, unfortunately, gave the white marble concrete too much of a yellowish tint.

Siri Derkert's own texts between the drawings have the same somewhat random, topical and provocative character as the graffiti. Against the background of the station's cool and rather solemn atmosphere, some critics found it inappropriate. Anders Åman wrote in a *Svenska Dagbladet* article, 20.9.65, that "the use of monumental art in the underground means an inbuilt obsolescence which all too soon becomes really annoying, since it lacks any kind of context in this station.—Östermalmstorg is that very strange phenomenon, a daily newspaper in concrete." Siri Derkert replied three days later in the same newspaper: "It is possible but unlikely that some names will be forgotten, but there is more than just names here. Around Rachel Carson is a picture of spring, nature and love. The main point will never be forgotten—the contribution she

Siri Derkert engages Helge Berglund and Hjalmar Mehr for the first waltz at the inauguration of Östermalmstorg station, 1965.

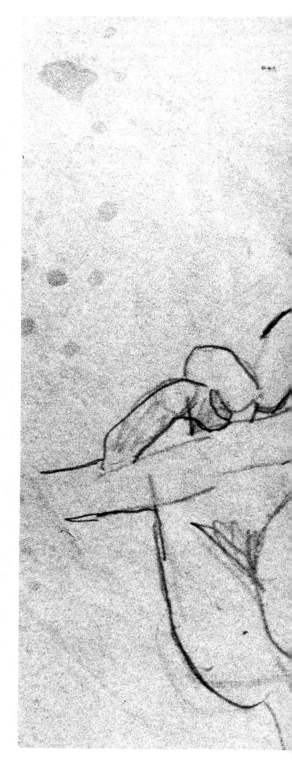

Siri Derkert: Detail sketch for "The Flautist" at Östermalmstorg station.

made for the protection of nature round about us. In any case, the aim is achieved if observers simply grow curious and go home to find out who Rachel Carson was and what she did.—No, what I am talking about will have lasting value. It has been relevant for far too long already. They should have carved words like these into all walls long ago. They could have started in 1789, for instance 'Liberty, fraternity, equality.' Have those things come about yet? Fraternity?''

Östermalmstorg station is without doubt the artistic highlight to emerge during the days of von Heland. At the same time, the somewhat sophisticated elegance and the rather difficult drawings and texts meant that the station was anything but popular in its appeal. One can understand Siri Derkert's view that the ever-increasing graffiti placed her work of art in a popular context which appealed to her rather more than the rarified elegance of the original background.

Three stations were to be without advertising, in accordance with the programme set out in section one of the competition. The other first-prize winner, Berndt Helleberg, was given Hornstull station as the location for his "Altamira Cave". The sparse but powerful imagery on the walls alongside the track in Dutch hand-made and glazed tiles in brick-red, white and black have points of contact with Siri Derkert's gougings. The consistently-planned whole can doubtless be regarded as the artist's finest work.

The third station where no advertising is allowed is Mälarhöjden, where Margareta Carlstedt's two 145-metre-long enamel paintings, "Ebb and Flow", finally ended up. She was 46 years younger than Siri Derkert and 14 years younger than Helleberg, and thus represented a quite different generation—but, needless to say, a much less experienced one. Her gigantic paintings take the form of a markedly abstract depiction of nature in clear colours, and are a sort of aquarelle painting against a light background: single strokes are 20 metres long, running continuously over a series of small sections. It creates the atmosphere of a heady summer's day, but naturally enough it is impossible for both the viewer and the artist to maintain

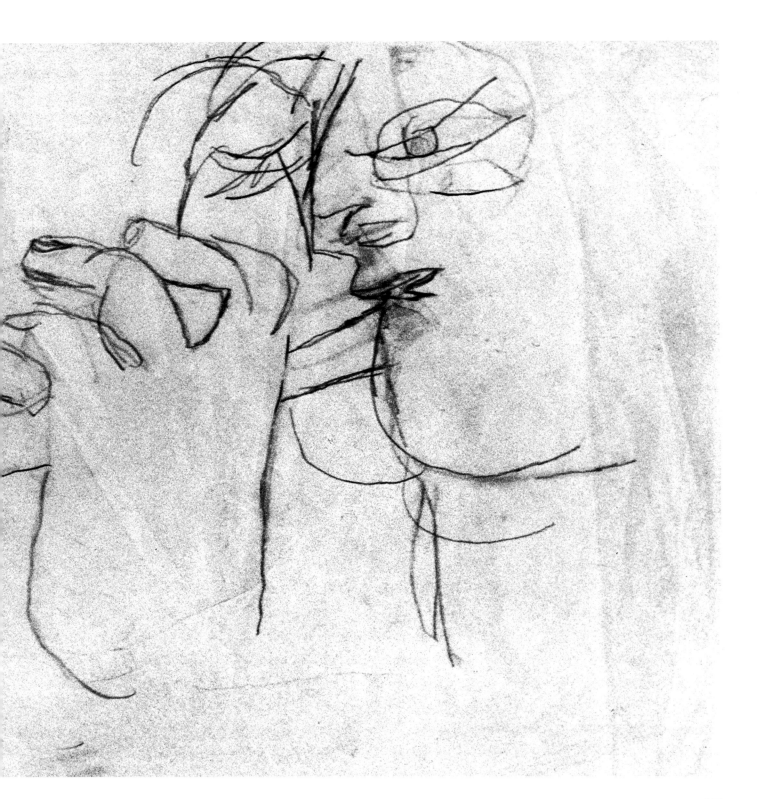

interest at a maximum for the whole of this 290-metre-long composition.

The enamel proved to be rather problematical from a technical point of view. The individual sections acted as sounding boards and amplified the noise of the trains until they were fitted with sound-absorbing material on the back. They were also vandalized rather a lot in the early days, and as a result the Tramways Company avoided using enamel in the underground until new, stronger enamels were produced by the Gustavsberg factories in the 1980s.

Karin Björquist's and Kjell Abramson's winning entry in group 2 of the competition was intended for a station where there would be advertising hoardings on the walls alongside the track. The original proposal had envisaged the ceramic decoration on the platform walls, opposite a series of cultural posters on the walls alongside the track. In fact the station ended up like the other stations on this line where advertising was allowed, and was provided with a long, blue strip intended for posters, the idea being that it would be filled with advertisements in more or less the same way as happened at the first subterranean stations in the Söder district in 1933. There was not much interest in renting advertising space in stations not right in the city centre, however, and for a long time the advertising strip was almost bare. Eventually, the Stockholm Transport Art Advisory Council hit upon the idea of replacing advertisements by so-called "loose pictures", that is, specially painted pictures from their collection. Once that was done, Mariatorget became one of the most highly praised stations on the old network. Here too, when the newspaper stand was closed down in 1978—79, the resulting wounds were patched up by commissioning the original artists to make a design for the empty space: two moss-green compositions in ceramic tiles with vegetable shapes.

In 1963—66, Slussen was at last awarded its first piece of artistic decoration from among the prize-winning entries in the competition, located in the new staircase leading up to Hökens gata. Aston and Birger Forsberg collaborated on the concretist deep-relief "Entrance Fee 70 öre", in yellowish white marble concrete; it is

Margareta Carlstedt: Sketch for "Ebb and Flow".

rather a subtle and sophisticated play on shapes, and was ready in 1966. Aston Forsberg was also responsible for a lattice of iron-shod flat balusters in light plaster, separating the platforms in the approach to the staircase where there is a difference in levels. Sune Fogde was among the prize-winners in the first competition, and in 1964–65 he was at last commissioned to produce a mural in one of the higher pedestrian walkways: irregularly shaped enamelled plates painted in strong colours fit into an abstract composition made up of patches of white, red-brown, black and yellow-ochre plaster, with the theme "Upandown"—the Swedish title "Opponer" contains several untranslatable puns.

Two more non-integrated works of art were commissioned, one in the pedestrian subway under Birger Jarlsgatan from the Östermalmstorg station and the other in the ticket-hall at T-Centralen facing Sergels torg. K G Bejemark's sculpture round a central pillar under Birger Jarlsgatan, "9 o'clock", depicts playful human figures formed by rough wooden shapes—it was originally conceived in copper plate. The original shapes have been modified in rather radical fashion as a result of scratches and carvings made by knives in the hands of passers-by unable to control their urge to meddle.

Sune Fogde: Sketch for wall in shaped enamel and plaster. Slussen station.

Staffan Hallström's large and beautiful stoneware wall in the ticket hall at Sergels torg, made at the Gustavsberg factories in cooperation with Lasse Andréasson and thought to be the world's largest stoneware mural at 35 metres long, came to an ignominious end. Some years after it had been finished, it was decided to build a public lavatory in the new House of Culture, where the reading room is now situated. Pontus Hultén, head of the state-run Museum of Modern Art which was then intended for location in the House of Culture, protested vehemently. A new site had to be found urgently, and the only possibility was behind the wall in the ticket-hall where the stoneware mural had only recently been completed. The artists protested just as vehemently at the proposal to make a lavatory door in the middle of their mural, and pointing to a clause in their contract insisted that the whole thing should be demolished. The Transport Company then sold the work of art to the Highways Commission for its original cost price, intending to use the money as

payment to the artists for a new work at another station. Eventually, however, the artists gave permission for part of the stoneware mural to remain in place, with a notice to the effect that it was only a fragment of the original work, originally entitled "In Anienes' Myrtle Grove" but now called "Clouds and Bridges". This led to the fragment being bought back by Stockholm Transport, at a greatly reduced price. It is now situated behind the glazed season-ticket counter, and is practically impossible to see.

Arrangements for the artistic decoration had been made in very informal and unbureaucratic style, thanks to Hans von Heland's great enthusiasm and the ease with which he was able to cooperate with the artistic advisers of the Tramways Company, often over dinner at von Heland's home, or at the famous restaurant Den Gyldene Freden. The Art Advisory Council, originally formed on Hjalmar Mehr's initiative in order to give artists an opportunity of counteracting what he saw as inertia in the Transport Commission,

Staffan Hallström and Lasse Andréasson:
Sketch for stoneware painting.
T-Centralen station.

had rapidly become an institution inside the company and, at the latter's request, had its remit extended by the Stockholm City Council in 1959. What had been the remains of a temporary prize jury became a permanent institution, completely independent of its former parent body, the artists' organization KRO.

When the underground network was extended further, the artistic design at the Karlaplan, Gärdet, Ropsten and Skärholmen stations had to be decided upon. The Tramways Company was sceptical about organizing another unwieldy competition so soon after the previous ones, especially as such a competition was unlikely to produce many new names among the entrants. It was suggested that a closer look at prize-winning entries from the other two competitions might be a fruitful way forward. The alternative was to approach artists direct and invite them to work on a particular station, possibly in competition with others. This way of doing it had been tried in connection with a number of small commissions, including Aston Forsberg's lattice at Slussen station and Carl-Axel Lunding's concrete frieze with shallow reliefs on the upper parts of

the walls around the ticket offices at Liljeholmen station, both of them personal commissions awarded in 1962 and completed two years later.

It was decided to thank the company's artistic advisers, who were not able to take part in the competitions, of course, by offering them a station each to work on. X:et declined on grounds of ill health, and Bror Marklund was not prepared to commit himself to such a big undertaking. Ten years later he was asked by the Stockholm Transport Art Advisory Council to decorate the Kungsträdgården station, having been one of the artists to submit sketches; but he was forced to decline on health grounds. Tor Hörlin had already received several personal commissions from the Tramways Company, including murals in structural clinkers in the pedestrian tunnel leading to Klara Church in 1964. He now agreed to make sixteen mosaics in the same material for the platform walls at Karlaplan station. The skilful architectural design with eight seating alcoves on each side, each one in appropriate colours and with varying, highly stylized naturalistic motifs, gives the station an especially pleasant and well thought-out atmosphere, and there is no sign of vandalism.

Karl Axel Pehrson agreed to decorate the Gärdet station, and proposed large, colourful, fantastic insects in glass show-cases along the platform walls. For years he had been passionately interested in collecting exotic beetles of the most varied kinds, and was now tempted to extend his own large collection by adding lots of new fantastic species, all with appropriate Latin names and descriptions. As many as 246 beetles, fantastic in both shape and colour, were placed in 36 glass cases along the platform. Unfortunately, these splendid little objects soon attracted the light-fingered, and after a store of spare beetles had been exhausted, more and more had to be replaced by photographs of real beetles from his own collection until in the end more and more show-cases were empty.

In 1965, the same year that members of the art advisory panel received their commissions in recognition of services rendered, von Heland retired and was succeeded by his own Commissioner, who was also chairman of the Tramways Management Board—Helge Berglund. Until the Stockholm Transport Art Advisory Council assumed responsibility for the task, only one commission was awarded apart from the special compensatory one for Staffan Hallström: art work for Ropsten, a partly open station, in 1971. The commission went to Roland Kempe, who had been invited to submit proposals in 1969 together with Margareta Carlstedt and Berndt Helleberg. Apart from a few small paintings in the pedestrian subway leading to Hjorthagen, the art work consists mainly of an enormous red, white and black snake, wriggling violently along the back wall of the platform with an arrow-shaped head at each end, pointing towards the trains. The original snake was painted out-of-doors with plastic paint, and soon began to flake; it was restored during one of the restoration sessions organized periodically by the Stockholm Transport Art Advisory Council. The artist employed to do the work changed and, in her view, improved the basically simple snake-figure; but it recovered its original appearance at a later restoration session.

The period from the end of the first competition in 1956 to the

Roland Kempe: Snake at Hjorthagen station.

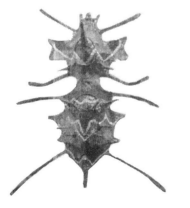

Karl Axel Pehrson: Beetle at Gärdet station.

setting up of the Stockholm Transport Art Advisory Council by the Greater Stockholm Council in 1971 was characterized by a remarkable change in attitude among the management of the Tramways Company. At first, they were sceptical about art in the underground and preferred to let the environment be shaped by the market forces of free advertising, but they came round to a marked commitment to the contributions made by artists, and were generous in providing funds so that the artistic intentions could be realized. Hjalmar Mehr, the chief supporter of art in the underground in the world of politics, had argued eloquently for laymen to have a say in the selection of artwork, suggesting that local politicians should play an active part: but the influence of laymen was by now negligible. The main responsibility had come to rest on a small group of established and discerning artists working together with the architects and the management of the Transport Company, who were becoming increasingly enthusiastic. Although the ideological background to art in the underground was the democratizaton of art, there was a fair amount of truth in criticisms suggesting that underground art was elitist in character.

The Stockholm Transport Art Advisory Council and the new underground

On 15 February 1971, the new and enlarged county council for the Stockholm area decided to set up three art advisory councils in order to distribute money allocated for artistic decoration: a central art advisory council, and one for each of the two most important areas of local government, the health services and public transport. As a result, the executive committee of the county council appointed seven full members and seven deputy members of the Stockholm Transport Art Advisory Council. As was normal practice for such bodies in Stockholm, deputies were to be invited to attend meetings and to take part in the routine work of the council, but they would not be allowed to vote unless full members were absent. In practice, there was virtually no difference between full members and deputies, since they did more or less the same work and there have been very few votes taken in the history of the Transport Art Advisory Council. It had been usual in the past for this kind of art advisory council and prize juries to have several members nominated by KRO, the artists' organization, but now they were only required to nominate one full member and one deputy; they were to take an active part in discussions regarding assessment, but were not allowed to be a party to decision-making. In this latter respect, therefore, the Stockholm Transport Art Advisory Council was in effect a lay body, although its formal function was simply to advise the Transport Commission, later to become Stockholm Transport (SL).

On 8 June the council had its inaugural meeting, at which Bror Hillbom, now head of the County Council's transport office, chief engineer Bertil Linnér and the new chief architect for Stockholm Transport, Michael Granit, among others, reported on current work and future plans regarding the extension of the underground network, and also what had been done in the past to introduce art into the underground stations.

The delay was no doubt partly to do with the scepticism of many at Stockholm Transport regarding the new advisory council and its role in an area which had become a source of pride for the company. Granit and his right-hand man (and eventual successor), Per H Reimers, had just worked out a completely new and different model for the new stations which was to be tried out in the rock station at Masmo, with Staffan Hallström and Lasse Andréasson as artistic advisers. Stockholm Transport had its own, admittedly dormant, art advisory panel, consisting of leading artists. They no doubt felt they were quite capable of dealing with such matters themselves in the forseeable future. Moreover, was a politically appointed advisory council an appropriate forum for discussions on something as unbureaucratic as art?

There were two quite distinct groups in the new advisory council: one consisted of more traditional politicans of an older generation (although they might not have been physically older), and the other of knowledgeable and artistically radical members with definite views on art and an eagerness to play an active part. The chairman was a County Council transport commissioner, assisted by Bengt Westerberg, who was later to become leader of the Swedish Liberal Party. The vice-chairman was also a heavy-weight politician of the traditional kind. Two members of the other group had more professional contact with art, an architect and an art historian; others had art as a hobby. Several of the council members had previous experience of working on more traditional kinds of art advisory panels. Politically, members covered the whole spectrum from conservative to socialist, but it is characteristic of the Stockholm Transport Art Advisory Council that its work has never been coloured by political considerations.

There were obvious differences between the traditional politicians and the rest, even if they were not as yet deep ones. One of the most significant local events in 1971 was the battle over the elm trees: ostensibly it was about the fate of an overgrown but cherished clump of elms which were in the way of entrances to the underground earmarked by the planners, but in fact it was a case of the man in the street versus his official representatives, who were accused of acting in accordance with their own private inclinations rather than carrying out the will of the people. There was now a desire among ordinary members from all parties to assert themselves as representatives of the people, while it was noticeable that established politicians were wary of anyone who seemed to be too enthusiastically committed and questioned the familiar way of doing things. Two of the council members represented the recently formed Cultural Workers' Social Democratic Association, the aim of which was to attain artistic ends via the political parties.

By 1971, many artists had grown tired of their role as drawing-room decorators in both a literal and metaphorical sense; the very phrase "artistic decoration" was beginning to sound stale. Socially aware artists around 1968 wanted to be a part of everyday work and everyday environments, they had no desire to become peripheral and use their "decorative" talents to try and beautify a technocratically designed standard environment which did not pay sufficient attention to the people who had to live in it. Artists played their part as consultants in the design of new housing developments, and leading architects such as Peter Celsing employed painters and sculptors in their architectural firms.

The first meetings of the Stockholm Transport Art Advisory Council discussed these very matters: the possibility of artists contributing to the overall design of stations, giving each station an identity in harmony with the local environment and the people who lived there, and giving an efficient transport system a human face. Stockholm Transport and the traditional politicians on the council were very suspicious from the start, and wanted to place firm restrictions on the areas which artists and the Art Advisory Council would be allowed to influence. Commenting on the council's proposals regarding its terms of reference, Stockholm Transport felt that the council's remit should be limited to *artistic decoration*, and exclude such matters as colour schemes, choice of colouring materials, and other architectural questions or points concerning fittings. Stockholm Transport wished to retain the right to *procure* proposals regarding decoration (i e choose which artists should be approached, as they had done in the past), once the council had reached a

113

decision about *what* should be decorated. When it came to assessing the proposals received, Stockholm Transport proposed to turn to their own art advisory panel. The advisory council would have no say in the actual carrying out of the work, which would be covered by a contract between the artist and Stockholm Transport Limited.

Despite these setbacks, an atmosphere of constructive cooperation was soon created—and the credit for this must go mainly to Bror Hillbom and Bertil Linnér who, together with Michael Granit and others, were members of a panel of experts attached to the advisory council at the suggestion of its chairman. Both of them had experienced the unbureaucratic and positive approach to artistic matters in the days of von Heland, and managed to bridge the gaps in confidence. By February 1972, the panel of experts was able to make proposals about terms of reference which corresponded in the main to the advisory council's wishes. The Art Advisory Council and the working parties it decided to divide itself up into, would work together with Stockholm Transport to produce definitive plans for artistic decoration, while the responsibility for putting those plans into practice would lie with Stockholm Transport in consultation with the Art Advisory Council. It was also proposed that decoration should in the main be restricted to subterranean areas, and that competitions would not be used as a means of contracting artists.

A question which attracted much lively discussion in these early stages was the role to be played by advertising. Granit, the architect, and the representative of the artists' organization KRO, were very negative towards all forms of advertising, as were some members of the council, while others were less antagonistic. In time it became clear that the question was a theoretical one as far as most stations were concerned, since there was little demand for advertising space in stations not right in the centre of town.

A total of 15 stations were opened between then and 1975; one on the Botkyrka Line (Alby), three on the Täby Line (Stadion, Tekniska Högskolan and Universitetet), and eleven on the Järva Line. All the stations were at an advanced stage of planning, espe-

Walls and roof clad in coloured metal mesh at Tekniska Högskolan station.

cially of course Stadion and Tekniska Högskolan, which were due to open in 1973. Stockholm Transport was chary of interfering with stations for which the planning was complete and where, in some cases, the contracts were already signed.

The projected new model stations
In order to understand the circumstances obtaining at the time, it is necessary to recapitulate the way in which the new underground was designed. There are three basic types of station: open stations (in the suburbs and on the outskirts of the city centre), concrete stations in the form of shallow concrete caissons, and rock stations. The oldest stations had been mainly of the first two types, but refined blasting techniques and improved methods of communication between platforms and the surface meant that stations could now be sunk deep into the high-quality Stockholm bedrock. The older rock stations, however, all had an inner coating of concrete and brick forming a shell which was often clad in some form of ceramic tile or other ceramic material on the walls. New developments in blasting techniques had now made it possible to construct

even suburban lines underground without escalating costs unduly, and thus avoid disrupting normal surface traffic. To reduce the cost of the stations themselves, however, it was decided to do without the inner shell of concrete, which was really unnecessary, and simply to coat the rock face with a skin made up of layers of sprayed concrete incorporating drains to prevent dripping water. It was felt, however, that the resultant caves would have an off-putting effect, and the architectural department of Stockholm Transport had experimented with designs incorporating a transparent wall of metal mesh instead of the concrete skin. The escalator walls were also to be lined with similar material.

The Art Advisory Council was very sceptical when it heard about plans to line walls with metal mesh panels. Would not the resultant cage-like enclosures be even more off-putting than the bare rock face? Later on, when the council visited one of these caverns, members were impressed by the grandeur of it all and wondered whether it was really necessary to conceal the rock face. Despite the council's objections, however, the plan to line walls with metal mesh panels fitted with moveable display frames for advertising posters was retained as the basic standard pattern for all stations. In December 1971, Granit presented a discussion paper on art in underground stations based on this fundamental design.

Variations in visual impressions were necessary in order to achieve visual stimulation, and it was felt this could be achieved by such means as removable prints, posters, lighting effects, mobile lighting arrangements, occasional exhibitions, new purchases every year, movable screens, and higher standards governing the artistic quality of posters and advertising. Apart from the removable pictures, however, it was suggested that art should be placed in position permanently, one reason being the proposal that it should have motifs with local links. To ensure a sufficient degree of variation from station to station, it was suggested that each one should have a group of four or five artists to work in conjunction with the architect and any other people involved to establish the choice of motifs, the colour scheme, the materials from which the works of

Staffan Hallström and Lasse Andréasson: Playing Card. Sketch for decorating the metal mesh at Masmo station.

art would be made, etc. Interested artists should be given the opportunity of submitting suitable photographs of their work as well as other references and a written justification of what they were proposing to do. Selections and the establishment of groups would be done in consultation with Stockholm Transport's Art Advisory Panel and possibly experts in the field who might be coopted.

The programme signified a clear departure from the all-too-final and solemn kind of decoration characteristic of the previous build-

ing stage. It proclaimed great interest in cooperation with various kinds of artists, but left little scope for contributions from the Stockholm Transport Art Advisory Council. It is quite obvious that the starting point was the cooperation involving Staffan Hallström and Lasse Andréasson at the Masmo station, which was shortly due to be opened—the commission awarded to compensate for the spoilt stoneware mural in the ticket hall at Sergels torg.

In fact only the Masmo station, the designs for which were already complete, came into being entirely in accordance with Granit's plan for a typical station pattern. The first two stations to be completed with the Stockholm Transport Art Advisory Council being involved, however, were strongly affected by the decision of principle made by Stockholm Transport to line walls with metal mesh panels. Two other important points did not lead to differences of opinion between the council and representatives of Stockholm Transport. In order to give each station an individual identity linked with local characteristics, the council considered it important for the artistic treatment to relate to some aspect of the station's catchment area, and so in the stations first on the list for completion, Tekniska Högskolan (the station serving the university of technology) featured technology and its history, while Stadion (serving the sports stadium) featured sport; in the old stations the artistic decoration was not linked specifically to a particular station and hence works of art could just as well be displayed in one station as in any other. The rather important question of principle concerned the organization of competitions. Stockholm Transport preferred to avoid open competitions because of the awkward and time-consuming administration involved, and also because of a general rule governing public competitions which forebade the discussion and influencing of individual entries before judging had taken place. The Art Advisory Council also preferred to commission several sets of sketches, since that avoided the necessity of declaring a winner and instead enabled assessors to choose freely among the proposals considered to be best out of several more or less equally good ones, and to make use of good ideas in other contexts.

The first working parties: Tekniska Högskolan and Stadion

As mentioned above, it was decided as early as the third meeting to make the work of the council more efficient by dividing up into working parties. Three working parties were established on 24 February 1972: one for the Tekniska Högskolan station, one for the Stadion station, and a general planning group dealing with "Other Stations", consisting of remaining members of the council apart from the presidium. The artists' representatives from their organization were included in the working parties in order to help with contacts with artists.

Michael Granit had produced several memoranda spelling out his view of the range of art work required, and how to organize the sketching stages. The council did not object in principle to his ideas about variation and diversification, but argued that one artist should have overall responsibility for every station, so as to avoid the negative competition between works of art which was noticeable at the old T-Centralen station: the artist given overall responsibility should be able to propose collaborators, should he so wish. Members of the council were keen to see the station treated as a total environment, integrated from an artistic point of view as a result of cooperation between artists and architects.

The two working parties linked to particular stations started out in a way which was to become the norm with very few exceptions: they first agreed on a theme for the station, and then selected a small number of artists who seemed suitable choices for carrying out the intentions. The artists invited to submit sketches were called "consultants", in an attempt to link the council's views on parallel commissions with the normal routines of art advisory councils; this terminology was not used again. Three artists were approached in connection with the Tekniska Högskolan project: the stage designer Lennart Mörk, the sculptor Per Olof Ultvedt and the painter Gösta Wallmark. Mörk's sketches were considered to come closest to the intentions of the working party, and the other proposals were passed on to the "Other Stations" group so that they could be taken into consideration in some other context.

To some extent, the choice of artists for the Stadion station was made rather differently. In accordance with a proposal made by the representative of the artists' organization, the painter Åke Pallarp was appointed "project leader" with an opportunity of coopting other suitable artists to assist with permanent decoration. As the station was located midway between the sports stadium and the College of Music, it was proposed that the decorative themes should be sport and music. Pallarp chose Enno Hallek as his partner.

Lennart Mörk based his designs on versions of the four elements, the laws of nature and the basic technological principles. His "stage designs" were profusely rich to start with, but as time went by they had to be modified on grounds of safety, maintenance and cost. These modifications were probably a good thing in the overall context, but there is no doubt that Stockholm Transport's insistence on keeping most of the metal mesh, even in the platform ceiling, had a negative effect. Important symbolic details, such as the detached wing of Ikaros and Newton's falling apple, disappear in rather ridiculous fashion into murky holes in the metal mesh ceiling. Pallarp and Hallek were more successful in exploiting the cave area itself which had captured the imagination of the Art Advisory Council. The metal mesh panels were removed from large areas of rock wall, which was painted sky-blue in the form of concrete fresco rather than the neutral grey of the sprayed concrete. This blue fairy grotto was given a small number of distinct and colourful symbols which also acted as station information. Here and there on the background of blue rock are various references to the world of sport: club badges, for instance, and an enlarged poster for the Stockholm Olympic Games of 1912. The connecting tunnel boasts a magnificent rainbow arching over the blue vault of the rocky sky. For the first time passengers had an opportunity of finding out just how beautiful and harmonious a rock station could be, simply by emphasizing its functional qualities and exploiting its natural features.

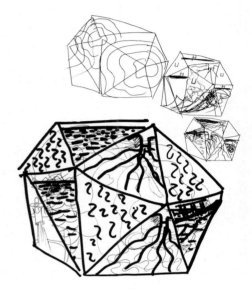

Lennart Mörk: Sketch for "Icosahedron".

120

The second stage of working parties

At the end of November 1972, the representative of the artists' organization KRO, Birger Boman, wrote a rather indignant letter to the council chairman and pointed out that on several occasions he had indicated the vagueness with which the work of the council was being conducted: "The underground network is being extended in accordance with a set timetable which cannot be tampered with. It is clear that important environmental, artistic and financial considerations are being put at risk, and the way the council is conducting its business, artistic work is being carried out under constant time pressure, or is actually being hindered because of this." He demanded that a master plan should be drawn up, showing how the artistic contributions to the new underground network as a whole should be distributed over the system, a financial plan showing how the expected allocations would be split among the various stations, and also a plan showing the time available for making the sketches and actually carrying out the required art work. With an eye to the future, he proposed the setting up of more working parties so that they would be all ready to design the next batch of stations when this task was passed on to the Art Advisory Council.

The "Other Stations" working party had spent most of their time discussing Granit's ideas about loose pictures, micro-art, and artistic variations on the theme of metal mesh and lighting; in fact, proposals for competitions featuring the first two points had been drawn up. It was now agreed that the working party had been a little too hasty, and instead two new working parties were set up, as proposed by Boman, to deal with the most pressing problems of the stations next on the list. One lesson that had been learnt by the first set of working parties was that the working method established by the council was extremely time-consuming. In 1972, the "KTH-Group", planning the Tekniska Högskolan station, had nineteen meetings at which minutes were kept—a task made no less strenuous by the fact that in the early years the chairman of the working party also acted as secretary, and as often as not was expected to type out his own minutes. In an attempt to economize on members'

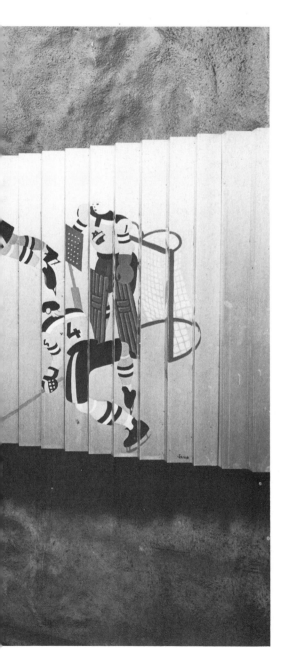

time, the two new working parties set up at the end of 1972 consisted at first of only two delegates, each with its own consultant from the artists' organization. Each working party was allocated three stations: one was given the city-centre stations Rådhuset and Stadshagen, and the new part of T-Centralen was added later; the other was allocated the suburban stations Rinkeby, Tensta and Hjulsta. Needless to say, the chief architect Michael Granit was an *ex officio* member of all the working parties, and he was often accompanied by his right-hand man Per H Reimers.

At the same time as these new working parties were being set up, the council's panel of experts produced a proposal for the categorization of stations now at the planning stage, with regard to artistic decoration. Bearing in mind the design of the stations and the planning stage reached, it was now proposed that two stations should have quite a lot of art work, that even permanent fittings should be affected, and that there should be pictures on the track walls. Seven stations were to have permanent and characteristic art work in certain areas as well as pictures on the walls alongside the track, while five stations would only have pictures on the track walls and some simple painting in accordance with the Masmo model.

In March 1973 the council invited Swedish artists and foreign artists active in Sweden to submit entries for a public competition "for the artistic activation of subterranean underground stations". The aim was to build up a collection of pictures as suggested by Michael Granit, to form a pool so that individual works could be exchanged or moved around from station to station. Stations were envisaged as following the Masmo pattern, where art was in competition with advertising posters.

A total of 241 entries and over 800 pictures were submitted, and 27 entries were awarded prizes. Despite the large number of entries, the overall artistic quality was indifferent. The appropriate working parties selected from among the winners pictures for the stations at Stadshagen and Hjulsta, which were still in group three. For Stadshagen the working party chose a sports picture featuring two ice-hockey teams painted simultaneously onto corrugated aluminium

by Lasse Lindqvist; a similar picture depicting two football teams was commissioned to go with the ice-hockey one. Needless to say, the choice of motifs was a reference to the Stadshagen sports complex, and the pictures were never intended to be moved. More pictures for this station were ordered later: two new sporting themes were commissioned and the old ones were extended in the form of pennants in an attempt to fill the enormous space more satisfactorily, and more were added in 1985. The pictures at Hjulsta were really intended to be movable, but they have in fact become permanent.

When Stadshagen and Hjulsta were opened, the lining of walls with wire mesh panels was no longer contemplated. Nevertheless, Stadshagen has a hangover from the original model in that its walls have retained the neutral dark-grey, granite-like colour in the cave area and the lighter streak in the connecting tunnel. On the imitation rock face, the various markings where the drainage channels have been inserted in the sprayed concrete and the registration marks normally made when a station area is under construction have all been repainted. The area has a cool architectural beauty, but makes a cold and rather inhospitable impression.

Svenolov Ehrén, Sigvard Olsson, Stefan Thorén and Olle Ängkvist were all commissioned to make sketches for the Rådhuset station. As far as possible the decor was to be linked with the various public buildings and institutions the station would serve, such as the civic centre, the town hall, the records office, the technical council centre and the municipal council chambers—or simply link up with the Kungsholmen district. The artists could, at their discretion, plan for the whole station, or for the platform area and the big pedestrian tunnel; it was also possible to split the work between two artists, working individually.

Of the four proposals, three had the desired links with Stockholm. The fourth, which was declared the winner, was by Sigvard Olsson and consisted of just three colour samples, four A-4 pages of text and a small compact of French powder. The main thrust of Sigvard Olsson's proposal was that the building of the tunnel itself

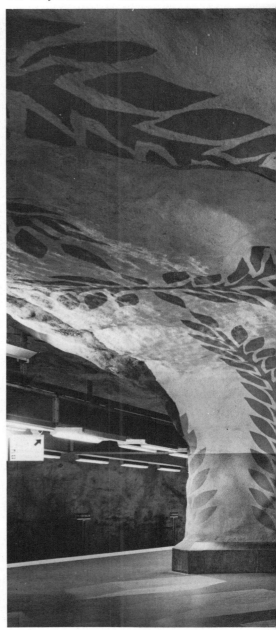

should be the work of art, and that a warm colour scheme should bring out the characteristics of the tunnel and make it a pleasant human environment. The subway from Parmmätargatan was to be painted a comfortable powdery pink colour and give the impression that people were walking through the heart of the Atlas Mountains. The Art Advisory Council decided that the proposal should be developed to take into account the original guide-lines. In his capacity as an antiquarian at the Stockholm City Museum, the chairman of the working party was able to negotiate with the museum and with its help, a plan was devised in which architectural features from the history of Stockholm grow out of the pink walls, rather like the buildings of Herculaneum gradually emerging as archaeologists dug them out. Two large items were to be cast and set up at the station: the decorative base of the old chimney from the Separator factory, which could still be seen outside the Tekniska Nämndhuset building, and the portal of Vadstena Castle, through which the trains would emerge into the station. Because of the shortage of time, however, the stucco firm entrusted with making these items did so as rather free copies. After the station opened, its decoration was added to by new castings and poetically informative signs, since neither the artist nor the working party was satisfied with the first version. The important thing about Sigvard Olsson's original design was that all the metal mesh should be removed so that the rock face could be as little tampered with as possible, and have maximum effect. Since the two previous stations had turned out well, any misgivings on the part of the Transport Company were soon dissipated, and work on this station was characterized by maximum receptiveness towards new ideas. The Architecture chapter described the internal conflicts and public criticism which had to be endured before the present stage was reached.

One of the proposals for the Rådhuset station, that by Olle Ängkvist, was passed on to the working party dealing with the Alby station, at the suggestion of Michael Granit. It was used, after some thorough revision: a constantly changing, almost non-figurative but nevertheless lively pattern in billowing, bright colours, flowing for-

126

ward to fill the whole wall space against a green background. This vast project drained the artists's resources, and he felt artistically washed-out for some time.

The working party recommended that Ultvedt's unused design for Tekniska Högskolan should form the basis for the decoration of the new part of T-Centralen. It was assumed the emphasis would be placed on a coordinating graphic solution for decoration, information signs and so on. A railing made by Ultvedt for the old station had disappeared as a result of re-building works, and that was another reason why he should be given another commission for the same station.

What was not realized was Ultvedt's ability to revise and renew an artistic creation constantly while working on it. The sketches he produced were not even remotely like his original submission thought by the council to be sufficient grounds for awarding him the commission. The great arches were painted with vegetative motifs in brilliant blue and white inspired by Gothic church paintings; the sacred patterns were occasionally interrupted without warning, however, by the imprint of tractor tyres. The working party was offered a choice between a blue and a green design, but apart from that the proposal was complete as it stood (the working party chose the green version, but Ultvedt later went over to the blue one after having seen the Universitetet station). The floor is very cleverly laid with multi-dimensional patterns in multi-coloured terrazzo. While the work was in progress, its scope was increased in accordance with the artist's suggestion, to include the section of wall alongside the tracks directly opposite the connecting tunnels, areas originally reserved for advertising.

Ultvedt had chosen a purely decorative design in the station area, so as not to tire passengers by foisting his personal views on them. One day, however, at the top of the escalators at the beginning of the passageway leading to the old part of the station, there suddenly appeared a rich and imaginative figurative work of art depicting in silhouette the workers and artists who worked on the station; one of the workers is smashing the notorious § 32 with his hammer. (§32

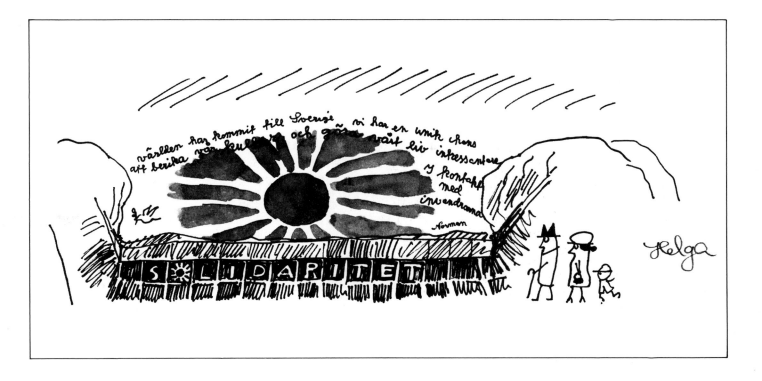

Helga Henschen: Sketch for Tensta station.

gave employers the exclusive right to control and allocate labour, and was resented by workers desiring participation.) This part of the decoration was as much of a surprise for the Art Advisory Council as it was for Stockholm Transport, but it was willingly approved in retrospect. It should be mentioned that the very modest fee paid to the artist, based on the original limited design, was never increased, nor did the artist expect it to be increased to keep pace with the size of the undertaking, which had increased on his own initiative. Over and over again, the artists working on the underground have voluntarily increased the scale of their contributions, so that when their payment is worked out at a rate per hour or per item, it has frequently given members of the Art Advisory Council nagging guilt feelings.

It was decided at long last to try and realize the idea of a gallery with paintings by various artists, so often put forward by the architects, in the connecting passage. It seemed appropriate to give the younger generation of New Realists an opportunity here, since their techniques made it difficult for them to make their mark on the gigantic scale needed when treating a station as a whole. From many possible candidates, four were chosen: Olle Kåks (who was put forward for Stadshagen on the assumption it would be moved into a higher group), Ola Billgren, Janne Håfström and Ulla Wiggen. Of these only Ola Billgren actually submitted a sketch for his old-master-like series of Christ-portraits, which was originally intended to have a post script with a socialistic motif. Ulla Wiggen painted polished sea-scapes from the outer archipelago with intimate family portraits, while Janne Håfström produced three triptychs, "a flood of images with memories from our own consciousness and the inside of the earth". Ola Kåks created twelve long, thin paintings reminiscent of wallpaper designs, intended to flicker past the gaze of passengers on the moving walkway. The 37 pictures arranged in 4 groups were never satisfactorily located nor lit, and unfortunately they soon became targets for theft and vandalism. Perhaps they were too sophisticated for this stress-laden environment. In the autumn of 1984 they were substituted by two long enamel paintings by Carl Fredrik Reutersvärd, a personal commission stemming from his proposal for the Sundbyberg station.

The other working party set up towards the end of 1972 worked away assiduously: in 1973 they had 21 meetings at which minutes were kept. Helga Henschen was selected without competition to design the Tensta station. Helga Henschen's station is dedicated to immigrants and has quite a lot of text accompanying the pictures: the text was carefully scrutinized by the Art Advisory Council and Stockholm Transport before being given the go-ahead, to make sure that nothing went against the strict code of neutrality insisted upon by the public transport authorities. Stockholm Transport was worried that the white surfaces incorporated in the original sketches would invite graffiti, and as a result Helga Henschen filled almost every acessible square inch with decoration instead, a gigantic task and one she did not find particularly satisfying from an artistic point of view.

As far as the other stations were concerned, it was decided that Hjulsta would be decorated exclusively with "loose pictures" from the competition. The Universitetet station was considered a little later, and Pär Andersson was invited to submit plans without com-

Pär Andersson: The exit leading up to Universitetet station.

petition from any other artist. His station incorporates motifs from the Norra Djurgården district and Bergianska Gardens, with plants in summer and autumn colours growing up all over the walls. The paintings are diffuse and non-figurative on the rock face, but on the makeshift wall surfaces that emerged from the final stages of construction they are lovingly figurative. This time round, the only station for which several artists were invited to submit sketches in competition with each other was Rinkeby, where John Wipp, Laris Strunke, Hans Wiksten and Nisse Zetterberg were approached. Nisse Zetterberg was asked to proceed with his designs, and he chose the painter Lennart Gram and the sculptor Sven Sahlberg to assist him. Zetterberg latched on to the many prehistoric finds discovered at Rinkeby, exquisite little objects magnified many times and reproduced in golden mosaic for the station. Gold mosaic is an expensive process, and the many mosaics in the original sketches were pruned down for financial reasons. The artistic effect is completed by Gram's large-scale bird paintings and Sahlberg's chandelier hanging from the roof in the form of a gilded ''Roslagen rose'' with petals in the form of oars. It was only when work started on the Södra Järva line that the station area could be completed—by Alf ten Siethoff—fully in accordance with Nisse Zetterberg's sketches.

The 1973 and 1974 Working Parties for suburban stations

In 1973, a new working party was set up to deal with the Alby and Fridhemsplan stations. As mentioned previously, the proposals made by Olle Ängkvist for Rådhuset were transferred to Alby, while Jan Brazda, Ingegerd Möller, Gunilla Palmstierna-Weiss and Peter Tillberg were all invited to submit sketches for Fridhemsplan. Ingegerd Möller was selected to develop her proposals, and she worked in cooperation with Torsten Renqvist on some sculptural details, notably an albatross sculpted in wood. The theme had no direct links with Fridhemsplan, but was linked with the archipelago —and more particularly the west coast skerries. The overall impression of the cave walls, where stippled effects in bright colours on a grey ground were supposed to suggest granite cliffs belching forth

Anders Åberg and Karl-Olov Björk: Showcase at Solna Centrum station.

132

colourful lava, were less effective than in the sketch, due to the enormous size of the walls. Jetsom displayed in show-cases and a genuine Blekinge skiff with a red sail were rather more impressive. The most attractive feature of the station is perhaps the gigantic pedestrian tunnels between the staircases leading out of the station, where real green moss on the bare rock face sometimes combines with artistic images of itself on the sprayed surfaces.

Another working party was set up at the same time for the stations at Västra Skogen, Solna Centrum, Näckrosen and Hallonbergen. It was decided to commission sketches for Västra Skogen from Curt Asker and Sivert Lindblom, for Solna Centrum from Karl-Olov Björk, Anders Åberg and students at the College of Art, for Näckrosen from Ulrik Samuelson and Lizzie Olsson-Arle, and for Hallonbergen from Gösta Wallmark and Elis Eriksson. Sivert Lindblom was given the contract for Västra Skogen; his design was considered best suited to the unusually large and complicated rock chambers; moreover, his proposed material was thought to be more resistant to defacement. Inspired by the name of the station, which means "Western forest", Lindblom evoked an atmosphere reminiscent of the cavernous chambers in Tolkiens sagas, articulated by his own well-known face profiles on a gigantic scale in black polished terrazzo and multi-shaped exotic tile arrangements; Ulrik Samuelson assisted with colour schemes for the latter. Under the arch between the tracks are small cast terrazzo shapes looking like abandoned skulls partly buried among what look vaguely like mounds of cobble-stones. The fence in black and coloured iron erected in 1982 to prevent people from running over the dangerous tracks has unfortunately undermined to some extent the atmosphere of a cult site.

Instead of submitting rival sets of sketches, Karl-Olov Björk and Anders Åberg decided to cooperate on designs for Solna Centrum. The sketches concentrated on models in showcases, several of them depicting old Hagalund motifs, and birds hovering freely near the escalators. The birds gave rise to some argument—Stockholm Transport's representative was one of those who expressed reserva-

Gösta Wallmark and Elis Eriksson: Murals and sculptures at Hallonbergen station.

134

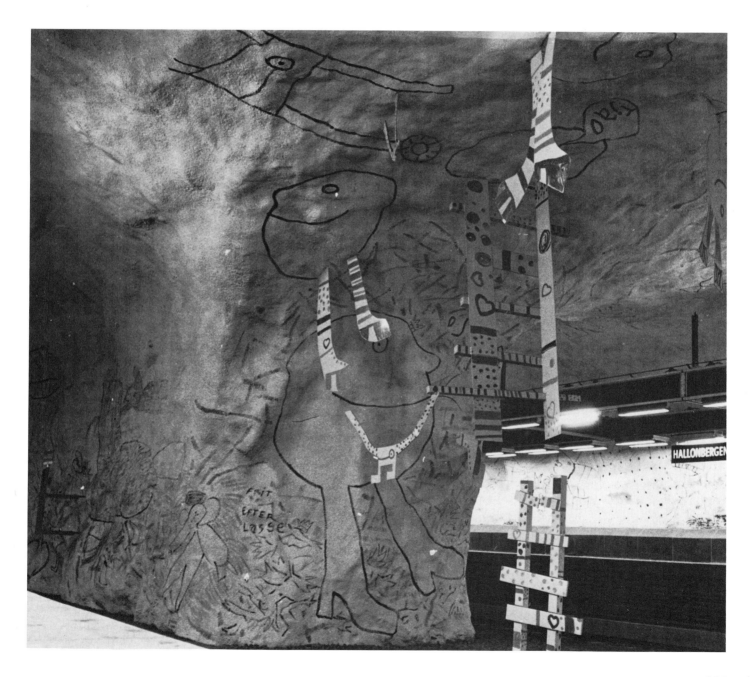

tions about the proposal—but in the end it was decided to go ahead with about 20 birds. On the walls, a symbolic green forest was to contrast with a red sky. While the work was actually in progress on site, the artists, encouraged by the workers, painted a series of engaging pictures from the Norrland countryside, linked by the forest motif—something not envisaged at all in the programme. Only a few of the models were produced, rather late in the day—after the station was officially opened, in fact; there has been no sign of the controversial birds, on the other hand. Unfortunately, several of the most subtle of the models have been badly vandalized over the years. Although the finished station has very little to do with Hagalund, the general public hardly seems to notice: they merely enjoy the old Hagalund atmosphere apparently evoked by the station.

Näckrosen also gave rise to a lot of discussion at the sketch stage, and revisions were requested both in the sketches and after development work had already been started by Lizzie Olsson-Arle. The final design was more closely linked with the film studios (located above the station) by introducing a series of showcases with cinematic memorabilia, and with the name of the station—"näckros" means "water-lily"—by means of a large, realistic painting on the roof of the connecting tunnel between the platforms.

As in the case of Solna Centrum, two artists decided to pool their efforts on Hallonbergen: Gösta Wallmark and Elis Eriksson—Wallmark had previously rented a studio in Eriksson's house at Hässelby. The starting point was Elis Eriksson's boldly naivistic but anything but naive sculptures on a large scale, complemented by enlargements of genuine or imitated children's drawings made by Wallmark, who actually did the work. Bertil Linnér tells a tale which claims that while the painting was going on, one of Stockholm Transport's inspectors went down into the station and, thinking children had broken in and scrawled all over the walls, took a paint spray and blotted out all the work that had been done so far. A painted fence was erected between the tracks in 1978—79 to prevent people crossing over from one platform to the other.

Hertha Hillfon. Female face, Danderyds Sjukhus station.

136

Birgit Broms: Vaxholm boats, Husby station.

In 1973, the "Other Stations" working party was also set up, and turned its attention to Bergshamra, Danderyds Sjukhus and Mörby Centrum. A proposal that College of Art students should submit plans was taken up in connection with Bergshamra station. Ten submissions were made, and one by Göran Dahl selected for putting into practice—but three of the others were thought good enough to be considered for the other two stations, although nothing came of the idea. Göran Dahl's design was centred on a new technique, with photographic pictures etched onto glass covering the rock face. An interesting variation on the arguments about the attractiveness of bare rock face is presented by pictures of the rock etched onto panes of glass covering the rock they are portraying. Kristina Anselm and Carl Johan De Geer also assisted with a couple of details, a book-train from the Soviet Union in the 1920s and a book-bus from northern Sweden in 1968. The station at Täby, which is full of rune stones, inspired the artists to reproduce runic inscriptions, although somewhat surprisingly they relied mainly on the mysterious Rökstenen in distant Östergötland rather than the well-known stones in nearby Uppland.

Hertha Hillfon and Ivan Jacobsson were asked to submit sketches for the Danderyds Sjukhus station, as was Curt Thorsjö, who had been involved in several similar operations previously but was unable to participate on this occasion. The job went to Hertha Hillfon, whose preliminary sketch was so complete it was not considered necessary to develop it further. She linked her design to the hospital ("sjukhus" means "hospital") and incorporated the names of medicinal herbs stamped into Höganäs clay, and the serpent symbolic of medicinal science into the terrazzo floor-tiles. From "The Mysterious Pillar", a woman's face surveys the floor area in front of the staircase leading up to the hospital. A design for the southern exit was later commissioned from Pierre Olofsson. The theme for the design was The Tree of Life, a motif suggested by local people, and Olofsson turned it into a concretist composition of the kind which "the men of 1947" had once envisaged as being ideal for the underground.

Pierre Olofsson was also a contender for the Mörby Centrum commission, together with Göran Nilsson, Gösta Wessel and Eva Wiltek; on this occasion, however, it went to Gösta Wessel, who joined forces with Karin Ek. The original proposal included large photographs showing the blasting of the rock chamber, with Lennart Nilsson as the photographer; this feature had to be dropped, however, on financial grounds. The final design is based instead on pink and blue-grey shadows on the rough, creamy-white rock face, as if shadows had been cast by spot-lights from various directions; large areas are screens in front of excavated shelters, and there are rows of vertical, many-sided shapes standing against the walls.

In 1974, a working party was set up to plan for three more suburban stations, Kista, Husby and Akalla. These stations were supposed to receive a lower level of artistic decoration—Kista was in fact a surface station of the type which had hitherto received no art work at all. The working party originally invited sketches from three artists for Husby and Akalla, but later increased the number to four: Öyvind Fahlström, Anders Fogelin, Erik Cedervall and Linda Lysell for Husby, and Birgit Broms, Stefan Thorén, Madeleine Pyk and Birgit Ståhl-Nyberg for Akalla. They also sought permission to invite proposals for artistic decoration at Kista, and suggested Lars Erik Falk (formerly a consultant acting for the artists' organization KRO on the Art Advisory Council) and Berto Marklund, adding later Carl Emil Berglin; all three were sculptors.

A prerequisite was that the works of art could be placed on an advertising strip, planned but never actually used, on the wall alongside the tracks at Husby and Akalla. The designs recommended for putting into practice were both conceived in this way for Akalla, but since that station is a terminus, the walls alongside the track are hidden for long periods by stationary trains, and it was suggested instead that the art work should be located on six smooth walls along the side of the platform, with shelters behind them. Birgit Ståhl-Nyberg's designs for this station depicting typical men and women were inspired formally by the socialist realism of Léger and

Ulrik Samuelson: Waterfall at Kungsträdgården station.

the late Matisse, and hence they could be realized in material more suited to their formal language: ceramic-ware fired in moulds, with plaster reliefs. The ceramic work was carried out under the direction of the artist at Karin Björquist's Gustavsberg studio.

Birgit Broms' design, a very long painting on aluminium of decorative birch trunks, was thought suitable for Husby. The sketch has one of the boats plying the Stockholm archipelago visible behind the trees—in the finished painting, this has become a whole fleet of brightly coloured steamships, a tribute to the pride of the Stockholm archipelago. It should be mentioned that Öyvind Fahlström submitted a written proposal based on technically advanced electronic wizardry.

Of the various proposals submitted for Kista, Lars Erik Falk's huge dynamic composition of girders, leaning at an angle of 73° and going right through the station roof, was most convincing. There was not enough money available, however, and Stockholm Transport was sceptical about its technical construction. The artistic decoration of Kista station became a continuing saga in the Art Advisory Council, and it was 1980 before it actually came into being. Its eventual acceptance led to art work being introduced into several other surface stations to coincide with rebuilding works, including Axelsberg, Bandhagen, Blackeberg, Farsta, Kristineberg, Rågsved and Västertorp.

Kungsträdgården

According to the outdated plans for the Stockholm City centre and transport systems, Kungsträdgården was to be the most imposing of the inner city underground stations, alongside T-Centralen. From the traffic point of view it was expected to play an important role as the destination for passengers from the new Järvafältet suburb as well as from Nacka and the south-eastern suburbs. As we all know, an attempt to press ahead with work on the Kungsträdgården station and the various alterations associated with it led to the big "Battle of the Elms", a turning point in the history of Stockholm town planning when local residents squatted in trees and prevented them being felled to make way for the building works. Despite the fact that after the Battle of the Elms it became increasingly clear the Nacka line would in fact never be built, and hence the station would be a rather quiet terminus, it still seemed appropriate to make it look imposing. Planning of the artistic design for the station started early, in the middle of 1974, and the working party was unusually large: in addition to four ordinary members of the Art Advisory Council, it included both the representatives of the artists' organisation KRO on the council, the architects Michael Granit and Per Reimers, and also Stockholm Transport's project manager Bertil Linnér. The working party proceeded in thorough and methodical fashion, and by the time the station was finished it had over 30 minuted meetings as well as informal meetings between artists and various delegates.

Ulrik Samuelson: Partly sawn elm trunk, a monument dedicated to "The Battle of the Elms", Kungsträdgården station.

Two themes were established by members of the working party. One was an attempt to reflect in various rather theatrical ways the effervescent cultural life taking place in the neighbourhood of the station, with its theatres, museums, musical events at St Jacob's Church, etc. The other was to link the design to the sculptured friezes preserved from the old Makalös Palace, which used to stand directly above the station, and the Kungsträdgården park itself, so rich in tradition.

When it came to choosing artists from whom sketches would be invited, the working party used a procedure which was to become usual for subsequent working parties: members put forward various names, and then the KRO consultants acquired slides illustrating the work of these artists and also others who might be worthy of consideration. After seeing a lot of slides and discussing the pros and cons, a vote was taken to produce five names of artists everyone agreed might be suitable to create art work in accordance with the themes laid down. Discussions about who to select took place on five occasions between 31 oktober 1974 and 15 January 1975, 11 working hours in all. The artists eventually agreed upon were the sculptor Bror Marklund, the painters Lage Lindell and Ulrik Samuelson and the stage designers Kerstin Hedeby and Acke Oldenburg; all of them had considerable experience of designing integrated environments.

Lage Lindell soon withdrew on health grounds, once he had seen the sheer size of the station; he also foresaw the damage which would quickly be done to a painted decor. And so, paradoxically enough, the enthusiastic champion of art underground never actually submitted even a sketch to the project, even though his artist colleagues thought they had honoured him with a prize in the 1956 competition. However, sketches and detailed motivations were submitted by the other four, and on 2 October 1975, the council agreed to the working party's recommendation that Marklund should be asked to make comprehensive sketches. He was doubtful about undertaking the task, partly because of pressure of other work and partly because of his advanced age; nevertheless, the council thought Marklund's proposal was by far the best, bearing in mind the requirements laid down, and asked him to reconsider. At its meeting on 19 November, however, the council was forced to accept that his decision was final. They expressed the hope that Marklund would undertake the task of decorating the eastern exit; it would be some considerable time before this area was ready, and it was thus taken out of the station assignment as a whole and shelved for the time being.

The invitation to submit more advanced sketches was transferred to Oldenburg and Samuelson, although the working party felt their rough sketches had not really followed the guidelines laid down in the remit. Oldenburg's proposal was based on coloured, form-cast, waxed concrete tiles, while Samuelson was working with green terrazzo for the floor and formcast seats, and the ceiling and showcases in glass painted from behind and set in a framework like that of a greenhouse—a design he had already used in his proposal for the Näckrosen station. The working party considered both designs to be too cold and insufficiently articulated, and so they discussed the requirements in detail with both artists before they went any further —glass was considered unsuitable for the station on technical grounds.

On 18 February 1976, the council finally agreed on Samuelson's thoroughly revised plans. Various cultural institutions were to participate by collaborating on both permanent and replaceable items, and a special working party was set up to oversee this.

For financial reasons, Ulrik Samuelson's very rich programme had to be cut back in certain detailed respects. On the other hand, various new and interesting proposals emerged as work progressed. The artist put a very great amount of work into the project, and according to his own calculations he worked about 2,500 hours between February 1976 and October 1977. Supplementary work was also carried out after the station was opened, such as patterns on the ceiling of the elevator shaft, and a decorative pillar where the escalator goes down to the platform. The art work is not restricted to the station itself but also spreads out into adjacent areas, such as a glazed snack-bar in the hall outside where Russian pasties are served. The work was carried out with the close cooperation of Per Reimers, the Stockholm Transport architect, and also the Stockholm City Museum, which assisted with castings of sculptures from the Makalös Palace and the roof of Riddarhuset (The Palace of Nobility). A special problem which was solved by mutual cooperation in a very elegant fashion was that the floor pattern in red, white and green tiles laid on the platform from various directions, did not match. The ingenious way in which the join was eventually made gave the whole area an extra quality. The station is a particularly well-executed example of how a total environment can be given artistic merit.

It goes without saying that the artist, who laid such stress on designing this total environment, was unwilling to let anyone else be responsible for the new eastern exit. The original decision made by the Art Advisory Council was invalidated, however, by the death of Bror Marklund, and so Samuelson, who had already started work on this section, was given exclusive responsibility.

Hans Bartos: Table and chairs,
Skogskyrkogården station.

Work creation schemes

Sweden has a programme of work creation schemes, and in the early days of the Art Advisory Panel it had contributed to the programme by providing work on artistic projects for the underground. In 1975, Hans Bartos made two gigantic armchairs and a table in heartwood for the surface station at Skogskyrkogården, and the same year Huck Hultgren produced a cheerful wooden sun and a bench in the form of a cloud with flowers growing from it at the Thorildsplan station, which is partly enclosed by Essingeleden, the urban freeway. In the spring of 1976, responsibility for this work was handed over to the Stockholm Transport Art Advisory Council, and it soon became one of its most work-intensive tasks.

Right from the start many people expressed reservations as to whether this kind of work was suitable for the work creation scheme programme. It was decided, however, that as a matter of principle the same qualitative requirements should apply to the scheme as would be laid down for art work in the underground commissioned by any other methods. When awarding commissions, however, the unemployment aspect would naturally play a key role.

Two kinds of work were decided on from the start: preliminary sketches for older stations, so that they were at hand when rebuilding programmes were launched, and "loose pictures" in the format used for advertising, more especially with an eye on the advertising strip which was hardly used at all in some of the older stations. Unlike the paintings in the connecting passage at T-Centralen, art commissioned for this project was required from the start to be able to compete with advertising posters on their terms—the works of art would be hanging alongside commercial advertising. The council also reserved the right not to display paintings unsuitable for the underground, on grounds of quality or for any other reason. The journal of the artists' organization, *KRO-bladet*, printed complaints from artists whose work had been refused in 1978—79, protesting about the Art Advisory Council's "censorship activities". Two stations were chosen for paintings: Mariatorget for pictures on the blue strip, and Slussen for the larger format normally used by advertisements. Many pictures were of very high quality, while others were relegated to the attics of Stockholm Transport where they were stored and kept available for possible usage in other contexts.

As a result of this initiative, the Mariatorget station has at last seen the realization of the architect Michael Granit's plans for a gallery of interchangeable paintings by various artists—despite the high costs involved, the pictures are changed at certain intervals. It is clear that the works of art are appreciated by users of the station, which is one of the most popular of the older stations. At Zinkensdamm station, however, where a few paintings were hung, the reaction was not particularly positive. It is evident that a station must have a full complement of pictures if the desired effect is to be achieved, and so the paintings displayed at Zinkensdamm were either moved to Mariatorget or withdrawn permanently.

Where "loose pictures" are concerned, every painting is regarded as its own sketch and is assessed retrospectively as suitable or

Sture Valentin Nilsson: Strindberg, sketch for enamel painting at Rådmansgatan station.

unsuitable for display. A good sketch can either be turned into a finished work of art as a result of the work creation scheme, as happened in the case of Gunnar Söderström's submissions for the Skanstull and Medborgarplatsen stations in 1979–80 and Matts Jungstedt's gate at Ropsten in 1980 (presented in sketch form in 1977), or it might be taken over by the Art Advisory Council for realization as part of its normal proceedings, as happened with Sture Valentin Nilsson's enamels on Strindberg themes, intended for Karlaplan but actually used at the Rådmansgatan station, which is located near the Strindberg Museum at Blå Tornet, the flat in Drottninggatan where Strindberg lived shortly before his death. A special working party was later set up for this project, chaired by Göran Söderström, who was also in charge of the Strindberg Museum. The enamels at Rådmansgatan were unveiled in 1983, at the same time as Larseric Vänerlöf's large-scale photo-montage on the old advertising strip at Karlaplan, and Casimir Djuric's concrete forest at the Vällingby station, both of which projects started out under the work creation scheme. Jan Forsberg's proposal for screened pictures of old Aspudden to be displayed at the Aspudden station was also taken over by the Art Advisory Council as part of their standard programme, but nothing has come of them, partly due to financial reasons.

The southern Järva Line

The last big, concentrated effort put into the decoration of new underground stations has been on the extension of the Järva line through Sundbyberg. This branch has four stations with a new design: a large, trumpet-shaped rock chamber with a platform in the middle. The largest station, however, Sundbybergs Centrum, has the same design as the rest of the Järva line. In 1977, the artists' organization KRO requested that an open, public competition should be organized to mark this last large-scale project. The council accepted the recommendation of a special working party that an open, public competition should be held for the four similar stations, while the normal procedures should be followed for Sundbyberg. Three working parties were constituted: one for Sundbyberg, which was to have most art work, one for Duvbo and Rissne, and one for Huvudsta and Vreten. The competition jury was to be formed by members of the latter two working parties, but the chairman of the planning group and jury was to be the chairman of the Sundbyberg working party. For reasons of manageability, the competition invited so-called portfolio-sketch entries. The regulations stated clearly that the organizers could not guarantee that prize-winning entries would be developed further, and that they reserved the right to choose freely and to invite new sketches if the competition failed to attract entries of a sufficiently high quality.

A total of 257 entries were received, of which 16 were awarded prizes and 6 were recommended by the jury for further development. The jury met on 14–17 and 29 March, 1978, during which time the various entries were considered and progressively eliminated in accordance with the usual voting system; unlike previous competitions, ordinary members, artists and representatives of Stockholm Transport all took part in the voting this time. The combined working parties for the stations under consideration decided to give two more prize-winning entries the possibility of being developed further, but did not consider it necessary to invite any further proposals.

The transition from portfolio sketch to large-scale execution gave several of the proposals a new and different dimension. It was a positive surprise to find that the competition led to commissions for all four of the stations. None of the artists eventually selected—the sculptor Gösta Sillén for Duvbo, Per Holmberg for Huvudsta, Madeleine Dranger for Rissne, and the Japanese sculptor Takashi Naraha for Vreten—had previously had anything to do with artistic projects in the underground. Sillén's station is a rarity: all the art is sculptural, with fantastic, half-human shapes growing out of walls and ceilings. Naraha's station, Vreten, is also characterized by sculptural shapes, prominent sky-blue cubes decorated with white clouds

Casimir Djuric: Wooden pillars at Vällingby station.

Lars Kleen: The Kronan crispbread factory. Wooden sculpture at Sundbybergs Centrum station.

in a refined composition, Japanese in character. At Huvudsta station, Per Holmberg has created brightly coloured tubes hovering over the platform like hanging gardens. Madeleine Dranger and Rolf H Reimers made a time-axis along the station walls and depict the short but eventful history of mankind and the fate of its various cultures in a cosmic perspective.

The situation at Sundbybergs Centrum was rather different, and more traditional. For practical reasons the other four stations had no given themes; for Sundbyberg, however, it seemed natural to link the station with the history of the town, without making the connection an absolute condition. The artists were chosen very carefully: after studying slides from the Swedish Art Advisory Council's collection, the working party selected 19 artists, both painters and sculptors, whose studios were to be visited. After doing so, the working party invited six artists to submit rough sketches—an unusually large number. The sketches were all of a high standard and very well produced, so the Stockholm Transport Art Advisory Council decided to buy all of them, for future documentation purposes. The artists concerned were Leif Bolter, Barbro Bäckström, Einar Höste, Lars Kleen, Carl Fredrik Reuterswärd and Björn Selder. Reuterswärd was given the opportunity of bringing his portfolio entry up to the same stage as those of the other contestants. Later on, Barbro Bäckström and Lars Kleen, the latter working together with Peter Tillberg and Michael Söderlundh, were asked to develop their proposals and make a large-scale sketch.

Before the proposals went to the council for a final decision, Carl Fredrik Reuterswärd's submission was brought back into the reckoning, and the final choice was between his and Kleen's plans. Kleen was the only artist to take up the Sundbyberg connection, and his design received strong support from the majority of the ordinary council members of the working party. Carl Fredrik Reuterswärd's sophisticated design, a blue enamel strip let into the rock face, was supported by the Stockholm Transport representatives and, the first time round, the chairman of the working party.

For the first time, a vote on the various proposals was called for in

Takashi Naraha: Competition entries for Vreten station.

the council. Half the ordinary members of the working party, the strongest supporters of Kleen's design with its local links—Sundbyberg houses from various epochs, full-size—did not have a vote in the council since they were in fact alternates. The chairman of the working party had the casting vote and used it to reflect the wishes of the alternates forming the majority in the working party, despite the fact that he had supported Reuterswärd there. The voting might appear to be paradoxical, but reflects the answer to the question: on whose behalf is art being brought underground?

There has always been unanimous support for the premise that artistic quality must be paramount when deciding on art in the underground. At the same time, the council has always striven to feature local links, and to encourage a design accessible for the vast majority. The experiment with paintings in the connecting passage at T-Centralen demonstrates that even high-quality art just does not work unless it reaches out to the general public.

The finished station at Sundbyberg's Centrum is characterized by Lars Kleen's fantastic abilities as a builder. The six examples of houses, five from the past and present of Sundbyberg plus a vision of the future, are masterpieces of craftsmanship, and this together with distortions of scale gives them an unreal dimension. Contrasting with the models are paintings, linked in their different ways, by the other two artists. The station has become a cultural landmark in Sundbyberg, just as envisaged by the majority on the Art Advisory Council in 1978.

A recurrent theme in the history of art in the underground has been complaints about the lack of time available for the coordination of artistic features with the overall design of the station concerned. In many cases, the shortage of time and advanced stage of the project resulted in stations with inadequate integration of the artistic features into the environment as a whole. Artists were commissioned for work on the Södra Järva line before building work was contracted out, a good seven years before the stations came into use. At first, it was feared that the artists might begin to lose interest during the long period of time before work actually began, but there were no such problems, even if designs naturally changed as the years passed by.

Even if it looks as though extensions of the underground network will soon be a thing of the past, the same cannot be said of artistic decoration for the stations. There are 99 stations in 1988, and art has been incorporated into 58 of them, mostly in stations north of Slussen. Sections of the network south of Slussen tend to be older, and made up mainly of suburban stations. There has been a constant stream of requests to introduce art into stations in all parts of the network, and demands for a more even-handed distribution of resources in general apply equally well to art on the Stockholm underground.

Once the Södra Järva line was finished, the attention of the Art Advisory Council has been concentrated mainly on adding a new dimension to older stations: efforts have sometimes been successful, but on other occasions the prospects have seemed so depressing even at the sketch stage that plans have been shelved for the time being. In 1980 Leif Bolter was invited to submit sketches for Axels-

Axelsberg station.

*Harald Lyth: Glass painting
at Slussen station.*

berg (he had previously been involved in plans for Sundbyberg), together with a group of artists combining to assist on the project: Veine Johansson, Inga Modén and Gösta Wessel. Their idea was based on a witty and varied depiction of the letters making up the name of the station. Their sculpted letters were in place on the slope rising up from the track by 1983. At Farsta, Gunnar Larson created a forest of treetops, hanging in the ticket hall, in the form of three-dimensional aquarelles and entitled "Transformations in the Sky". Jörgen Fogelquist, P G Thelander and Börje Lindberg competed for the Västertorp commission, and the former produced a mural depicting the engineer Andrée's flight to the North Pole by air balloon, "To the Pole with the Eagle". Both sets of sketches were commissioned in 1980, and the work completed in 1982.

Bringing art to the genuinely suburban stations has proved to be a problem. The most successful attempt is perhaps Freddy Fraek's outsize folding rule at Bandhagen, which from an architectural point of view blends in with Peter Celsing's design in a stimulating if somewhat "bold" way. Nevertheless, public response has not been especially positive. On the platform, the folding rule fits around a large 19-ton stone, which is a part of the sculpture, and in order to move it into place Stockholm Transport had to rent one of Sweden's largest mobile cranes and excavate a part of the embankment. The

The block of Öland stone is hoisted into place at Bandhagen station, 1983.

operation aroused a certain amount of interest despite the fact that it was carried out at night, and a young man approached Bertil Linnér to ask him what was going on. "I replied that we were lifting a large stone onto the platform. He gave me a long look and then said: 'What the hell for?' "

Several suburban stations have received some form of sculptured decoration. Björn Selder submitted his design for a mobile sculpture on the platform at Rågsved station, "Bird Green", an abstract bronze figure on a pillar seven metres tall. Unfortunately, the sculptor forgot to remove a locking pin when the mobile was set up, and so it remained stationary in the early days.

Many proposals emanating from local people involve a project carried out by themselves. Some Art School students organized the creation in 1979 of a large, colourful midsummer wreath in wood and a section of wall depicting historical motifs associated with the suburb Midsommarkransen, which means "midsummer wreath", for their local station. A work of art in the form of outsize jigsaw-puzzle pieces was produced for the Bredäng station.

At first nearly all the suggestions for artists to be commissioned came from the architect, the chairman of the working party and the representatives of the artists' organization. In some cases sketches were commissioned without competition, and so only those council members well versed in contemporary art were able to pass judgement on the quality of the submissions. In more recent years an effort has been made to give all members of the working party an

Björn Selder's sculpture "Bird Green" being set in place at Rågsved station, November 1983.

opportunity to pass judgement, using such means as advisory votes on a scale "don't like" "can accept", "like a lot" with points values of 1, 2 and 3 respectively. In order to sound out opinions on as wide a scale as possible, representatives of Stockholm Transport and KRO have also been allowed to vote—although the final responsibility has naturally rested with elected members from the Art Advisory Council.

In an attempt to assess the reaction of the general public to art in the underground, over and above the positive comments frequently made in newspapers and artistic circles, the Department of Art History at the University of Lund carried out a poll in 1981 involving detailed questionnaires and interviews inviting comments on the stations at Tekniska Högskolan, Solna, and the new T-Centralen. Results show quite clearly that the majority of all age-groups and all social and cultural categories regard art in the underground as a positive aspect of their everyday lives. The most highly-praised station of the three is Solna, which received almost exclusively positive comments from passengers of all ages and all categories. Although responses were a little more hesitant with regard to the other two stations, and more hesitant about the rather intellectual art work at Tekniska Högskolan than the rather solemn but nevertheless easily assimilated art at T-Centralen, the percentage of negative responses was quite insignificant.

This result would appear to be a rather positive judgement on more than a decade of cooperation between politicians, architects, engineers and artists in an attempt to create a more human environment for the travelling public, and confirmation that the vision which politicians and artists combined to turn into reality was no mere mirage.

Economy, maintenance, graffiti

Art in the Stockholm underground is financed exclusively by taxpayers' money. The grants awarded are not governed by percentage rules, that is, there is no general indication that a certain proportion of the building costs should be used for artistic purposes. The financial allocations depend entirely on the cultural ambitions of those in authority.

A question which always crops up whenever a new station is opened, when art is introduced into older stations, and when visitors are taken into the underground, is: how much did all this art cost?

It is difficult to give a straight answer and say that the art cost so-and-so many million kronor. Art has become a recognized part of the design and fittings for new stations. Of course it is true to say that the underground could have been built more cheaply if art, the collaboration with artists and good architecture had all been ignored.

When the T-Centralen station was to be fitted out and given its artistic decoration in 1956, the cost of the art work was calculated. The Tramways Company added together the fees paid to the artists, the cost of their materials and the amounts paid to craftsmen etc, and compared the total with the cost of the so-called standard design, taking into account the annual loss of income which would otherwise have been made from advertising. According to these calculations, the extra cost for bringing art into T-Centralen was just over 3 million kronor (all sums in this chapter are calculated at 1984 price levels).

As time went by and art became increasingly normal in stations, the extra costs were not worked out so carefully. Moreover, the loss of advertising income was more or less fictitious as far as less central stations were concerned, since there was very little interest in renting advertising space there. The extra cost of incorporating art into the underground during the period 1956–85, then, can be estimated at about 45 million kronor.

If the cost of the art work is expressed as a percentage of the construction costs, a comparison with the total building costs for the underground, some 9 milliard kronor, shows that the art work cost just over five thousandths of the whole. It is perhaps more correct to express the artistic costs as a proportion of the stations and their fittings alone, and this figure comes to a little more than 2 per cent. This is roughly the same as the standard proportion budgeted for by the Stockholm County Council when putting art into hospitals and such-like buildings.

How long can the art work in stations be maintained and renewed at reasonable cost?

It is not really possible to answer that question precisely, but the time is rapidly approaching when it must be given increased attention. Generally speaking, art in the underground is not representative, and it can thus be said it is quite timeless. There are some stations, however, where the contents are more dated, such as Östermalmstorg and Näckrosen.

How many young people of today know who Rachel Carson is, and who Östen Undén was, two of the many names inscribed in concrete at Östermalmstorg station? Many of the people Siri Derkert admired when she created her design, and to whom she gave historical significance, have now been succeeded by new names with devoted followings. At Näckrosen station, Lizzie Olsson-Arle created a tribute to the Swedish film industry, featuring Ingmar Bergman and other contemporary film-makers who achieved notable successes. How long will they be remembered by those of us who are not film historians?

When the underground stations were fitted out, attempts were made to use only durable materials and replaceable units. The first "wave" of artistic decoration in 1957 and during the 1960s had durability in mind and exploited ceramic materials, tiles, clinker, brick, enamelled sheet metal, etc. The cave stations of the 1970s brought with them coloured sprayed concrete as the main surface for walls and roofs. The concrete is sprayed directly onto the bare rock face in 80 mm-thick reinforced and drained layers. The sprayed concrete technique was new, but has proved to be reliable and

much cheaper than the concrete arches and ceramic cladding standard for the 1960s stations. Now that ten years have passed, however, it is clear that the cave stations are more vulnerable. Damp penetration, lime deposits and other deposits of unknown chemicals have resulted in these stations deteriorating more than others of a similar age. The deterioration has just about been held in check by continuous restoration work, using artists assisted by the work creation scheme, and at the same time graffiti has been removed.

The ceramic material in the older stations is more durable, but can involve problems when it comes to replacing it. Qualities and colours used 20–30 years ago are no longer being produced, and doing so would be prohibitively expensive.

It may well be necessary to renovate some stations completely in the next 10 years. The necessary work could prove to be so extensive and costly that a completely new design is the only realistic alternative. It is not impossible that a station might have to be gutted completely and redesigned in a totally different way. New materials and new techniques could well have emerged, making it desirable to start all over again in some stations – and this is a distinct probability in some places. As far as the art work is concerned, the contracts made with artists will not present any legal difficulties. In recent years, the artistic decor has been regarded as applied art whose existence cannot be guaranteed for ever.

Graffiti

A type of vandalism which many people regard as a reaction, is graffiti. A situation where art in the underground stations provokes graffiti must be exceptional. The inherent need many people have to leave behind visible traces of their presence would surely manifest itself whether or not there was art in the station.

To define graffiti as a product of artistic urges is not an easy task and fraught with ambiguity. But art is hardly ''legalized'' from an artistic point of view simply because it is planned and commissioned. The comments in the cartoon-type balloons at Hallonbergen and the deeply serious appeals for peace at Östermalmstorg

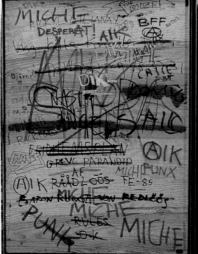

can surely not be regarded as special when judged as art just because they were written by well-known artists and commissioned by the local council?

Graffiti does not only have cultural-political implications, of course, but it also causes damage. Obviously, graffiti which has no other purpose than to do damage cannot be defended, nor is it easy to explain it. It is also clear that this type of graffiti is regarded very negatively by the majority of passengers.

Graffiti is more common in the Stockholm underground than in almost any other with the exception of the New York subway. As indicated above, many people distinguish between destructive defacement, which is simply vandalism, and graffiti with more artistic features. Defacement is regarded entirely negatively, while the more thoughtful kind of graffiti is treated with greater tolerance. People like to think of it as a cheerful and stimulating feature, a genuine expression of big-city life. Nevertheless, even this more advanced type of graffiti is a kind of defacement which cannot be accepted by the transport authorities and the local council. Stockholm Transport has decided to keep the underground clean and tidy, and hence any form of graffiti means expense. Erasing defacements in the underground stations costs approx 15 million kronor per year.

Destructive defacement is by far the commonest kind. Generally speaking, Stockholm Transport tries to clean up as quickly as possible: experience shows that this prevents it spreading. Scribblers hesitate to deface clean surfaces, but once a start has been made, graffiti spreads like a disease. The type of graffiti which displays a certain amount of talent, on the other hand, prefers clean surfaces, and then spreads quite extensively. Graffiti tends to appear in profusion for short periods, but can then die out completely for years on end.

The underground and public art

MAILIS STENSMAN

In recent years much more attention has been paid to the provision of art in more or less public places. Many local authorities have introduced a so-called percentage rule with regard to this question. The Stockholm County Council, which is responsible for the underground, decrees that up to two per cent of building costs must be spent on art work. In 1984 the government allocated a sum equal to one per cent of state building costs, amounting to almost 23 million kronor, to the National Art Advisory Panel. With effect from July 1985, 25 kronor per square metre—more than twice the previous amount—was allocated for the provision of art on housing estates. On top of this came private funding, donations etc.

Obviously, such sums make it possible to work on the artistic design of our public environments, work places, hospitals, schools, housing estates etc. A large number of works of art can be bought or commissioned—but unfortunately, the artistic dimension is usually considered far too late in the planning of a new building. The artist is thus deprived of the chance to cooperate with the client, the architect, the designer, the engineers, the users and so on. The possibility of contributing to a more comprehensive artistic design of the building concerned is thus undermined, partly or completely. If artists and craftsmen were to contribute to the building process, they could make our environment more stimulating in many and varied ways. Craftsmen could introduce solicitude and many different qualities besides making it possible to plan environments in ways which exploit a knowledge of colour, dimensions and traditions. Simple ornamentation, which can be witty and ingenious in its repetitions and the low-key signals it emits, could encapsulate space without generating a fear of emptiness.

Art does not necessarily mean the placing of a bronze statue in a square or entrance hall, with no thought being given to the context; nor does it necessarily mean a painting or a tapestry hung in the communal room of some building irrespective of its dimensions and colour scheme—everything decided at break-neck speed together with some consultant. Such things just happen to be there, often in rather absurd situations. Sometimes they stand out as a paradox, and occasionally they can be paradoxically good when looked at in that light.

Is this an illusion of artistic freedom? Or is it a sign of increasing dependence on commercial forces in the world of art?

The actual process of construction is so strictly controlled on financial grounds that it is difficult to discuss art meaningfully in this context, in view of its irrational nature. All parties specialize so narrowly and are so isolated from each other that one is sometimes amazed to find that planned buildings ever become real buildings in fact.

Even artists are specialists, isolated in their role as artist and not particularly well trained for the problems associated with modern building procedures. In recent years more and more attention has been focussed on art as a commodity, something to buy and sell and make a profit out of, and this together with the purging and impoverishment of architecture as a result of functionalism has created a gap in the tradition of caring about the upholding of architectural and artistic values. It may be that many artists nowadays lack the elementary ability to read and interpret architectural plans. Or they may have an anarchistic streak and don't even want to attend the many meetings necessary to get anywhere near the creation of an environment. And how can there be meaningful cooperation when the parties concerned don't meet at an early enough stage, or don't take one another's skills seriously? Do people really want cooperation to take place? Or do they regard it as a waste of time? Is art just something brought in half-heartedly as an excuse, to make things look a bit nicer, a colourful daubing in a project which didn't turn out too well, or even failed? Or is it more or less agreed that art in public buildings should just be something to keep the artists occupied, a sort of disguised welfare benefit to be distributed equally? Or perhaps distributed in a certain closed circle? Should the rest of us remain silent and not harbour expectations, express requirements or preferences . . .? The art critics

164

remain silent. An exhibition at a gallery or museum for a fortnight is duly reviewed, but a work of art in a public place, which has taken a long time to produce and has been seen by many people, is greeted with a deafening silence on the cultural pages of our newspapers.

Interesting work in public places has been done and is being done, and it should receive some attention and be studied as a stimulus to positive developments in a field which leaves much to be desired. Something unique has been created in the Stockholm underground. In various ways, artists have produced an environment, maintaining high standards throughout, and the results have gradually been developed until what we now have is an integrated total environment. How did it come about? Why is it that qualities have emerged underground which are seldom found on the surface? How did the decision-making and collaboration processes go? Did those commissioning the work come forward with clearly articulated requirements, based on expertise of their own? Was there a specific aim to be achieved? One could ask very many more such questions.

It is obvious that not only the finished products in the underground should be studied, but also the ways in which decisions were made and collaboration took place, since both these aspects are essential prerequisites if art is to be introduced into large spaces. However, if most of those involved in planning the incorporation of art into public places intend to continue with the usual pattern of painting little bits of canvas for hanging in galleries, or weave smaller and smaller tapestries for placing in public places, or make murals on odd bits of wall, when in every case the surrounding materials and colours are already fixed, then many people must see the working methods used in the underground as a threat. There, everyone involved was given certain requirements which had to be met, including the artists. The sacred period of creativity until the final sketches were completed was not a period of isolation, but discussions took place all the time and the skills, commitment and will of many people combined to develop the project until it finally took on its finished form. This is how the most interesting example of public art in Sweden this century, and one of the more interesting examples in the world at large, came about.

I have in front of me a pile three feet high of minutes, notes, various texts, records of conversations, etc., and it is soon obvious from them that those placing the commissions were committed to the project, and were very clear about their requirement that everyone involved should work together to create the best and most stimulating environment possible in these underground chambers. When work first started on the involvement of artists in the early 1950s, the concept of an integrated environment in the underground stations was not particularly well-developed. But several people believed firmly that art should somehow play a part in creating an environment for the benefit of the public at large, and they were prepared to fight for their beliefs.

The first stations in which art was incorporated do not display much sign of feeling for an integrated environment, although the programme laid down for the public competitions does project an integrated approach to some extent. Nevertheless, Östermalmstorg, for instance, which is one of the older stations, is a good example of an effective whole. This is no doubt due to the ability of the artist, Siri Derkert, to preserve the unity of the station area with regard to both content and form—despite the fact that the pictures give the impression of being casual scribbles, and consist of a series of individual works. The theme and the artist's burning enthusiasm enable the carefully prepared series of pictures to create a powerful effect which makes this station, finished in 1965, one of the very best. The recurrent musical notes in their staves hold the pictures

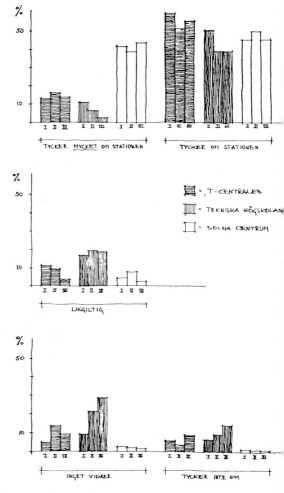

From *The Underground and the General Public, 1981.*

together rather nicely, besides combining to form a whole, a melody. Picture after picture, lined up like parts of a strip cartoon with captions, also derive strength from the artist's long experience and thorough study of the formal language of cubism and expressionism. It is not only the link with the somewhat violent speed associated with graffiti which gives this environment its powerful effect. That would belittle it. The real weight and power derive at bottom from the cry for peace, and the defence of our countryside, our world.

A new era in the history of art in the underground began in 1971. That was the year the Stockholm County Council came into being, and the same year the Stockholm Transport Art Advisory Council was set up together with two other similar art advisory councils. That was when cooperation started which was to result in the integration of art, engineering and architecture to form a unique and fantastic whole. Responsibility for the artistic side of things lay with the Stockholm Transport Art Advisory Council, which had several really knowledgeable and committed laymen as politically elected members. They started by defining principles, thus strengthening their position and creating a springboard from which collaboration could take off. The work of the council was undertaken in cooperation with the company responsible for running the underground railway, SL (Stockholm Transport). The company has a wealth of tradition and experience of working together with artists.

Work, commitment and skill are needed to make the underground environment as stimulating as possible. It's not a matter of going to the odd meeting, making decisions, then sitting back in the hope that everything will look after itself. From the very start, working on the whole cave area from an artistic point of view was an aim spelt out by the council. The basic idea, ''art for the people'', which had most recently become a slogan in society during the years around 1968, was a fundamental principle behind the work. Another was that artists should take part in the project on the same basis as everyone else, and contribute to the combined aim of a positive environment. A prerequisite if art was to have any real prospect of influencing the environment was that the artists should be involved at an early stage. Another basic idea was that the art created should be applied art, de-dramatized art.

The practical demands made of the artists were the same as for bricklayers, and this self-evident situation has been accepted by the team of workers at all stations as the years have gone by. This down-to-earth attitude has certainly been of vital importance, enabling the work to proceed satisfactorily and the results to be what they are. Given such working procedures, it goes without saying that everyone in the working parties takes an active part and develops his or her own particular area of expertise.

The positive reaction of the general public, shown by such things as opinion polls, jutifies the basically democratic approach adopted hitherto by the Stockholm Transport Art Advisory Council to incorporate art into public places for the benefit of the mass of the people.

Ulrik Samuelson: The eastern exit of Kungsträdgården station.

The Stations in Words and Pictures

T-CENTRALEN

The upper level of T-Centralen station, which was called Klarastationen in the 1950s, was the first one to incorporate art work. It was ready in 1957, and the art it contains was the result of a public competition organized in 1956.

Quite a lot of entries were given the green light, and a wide variety of items using different techniques were mixed up together, with no serious thought being paid to the overall effect. Before the contest took place, it was stressed that artists, architects and engineers should collaborate at an early stage in order to produce an

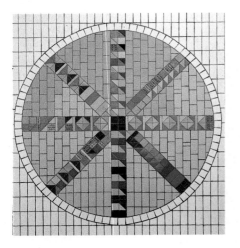

artistically coherent whole, but it was impossible to realize this intention since time was so short.

Twelve artists took part in the first stage of the operation, affecting the older parts of T-Centralen, with four of them working in pairs. Anders Österlin and Signe Persson-Melin col-

laborated on one of the 145 metre-long walls. On a base of white standard clinker, they produced a series of stoneware signs running in playful fashion along the wall at the side of the track. On the opposite wall, Erland Melanton and Bengt Edenfalk created "Klaravagnen" using multi-coloured glass prisms—the title is a play on words referring to both "coaches at the Klara station" and the Plough constellation. The pillars

on the two short sides of the station area, by Siri Derkert and Vera Nilsson, are the first works of art to greet passengers coming on to the platform. They seem small in the context of the enormous station, but the feeling of strength they impart is all the more effective when one realizes that the pillars are in fact supporting the weight of the roof. Siri Derkert used gouged concrete to create her pillar, which is known as "the women's pillar" since it portrays an oarswoman, a typist and a female bricklayer's labourer; the great writers Thorild, Almqvist and Strindberg are also invoked. Vera Nilsson calls her natural stone pillar "The Klara which refuses to go away". Close by are Egon Möller-Nilsson's beautifully shaped benches, sculptures for sitting on. The sculptor has made a name for himself on the basis of his outstanding sculptures for children.

The ticket hall nearest to the Central Station and the pedestrian subway

Two tiled walls by Jörgen Fogelquist adorn the ticket hall.

In the upper platform area are a concrete relief by Siri Derkert, a glass wall by Erland Melanton and Bengt Edenfalk, and sculpted benches by Egon Möller-Nielsen.

The upper platform area at T-Centralen.
Siri Derkert's woman-pillar.

The stoneware relief by Staffan Hall-ström and Lasse Andréasson has been partly dismantled as a result of altera-tions made at the Sergels Torg exit from T-Centralen. To the right is the Järva line platform area with the bright and light leafy decoration by P O Ultvedt.

leading to it were also part of the artistic programme carried out in 1957. The work of art in ceramic tiles on the two opposite walls is called "Return Journey", and was created by Jörgen Fogelquist: it gives the area a feeling of bustle and excitement.

Another platform area at T-Cen-tralen is part of the Järva line, and was opened in the mid-seventies. It is at a deeper level, excavated into the bedrock, and is quite different in kind from the older part of the station in that its walls and roof combine to form a single arch, thanks to new ex-cavation techniques. The shape of the original rock face is discernible behind a layer of sprayed concrete

some 7 cm thick. The surface is painted in blue and white (by P O Ultvedt) and is criss-crossed by leafy branches or creepers, reminiscent of the old murals to be found in provin-cial churches. Indeed, the connecting tunnels look like church arches. At the peak of the arch where the es-calators begin, a silhouette portrays all the workers who helped to make the station, and they form a cathedral of people hammering, painting, measuring, drawing, and smashing the despised § 32 with hammers. One never has a feeling of being op-pressed by the 26 metres of solid rock which is in fact between the platform and the surface. "I tried to create a

total environment, to decorate every-thing." says P O Ultvedt. "In my view it would be wrong to let the subjectivity of the artist obtrude in a job of this kind."

The passageway leading to the new Järva line was originally lined with a series of paintings by Ola Billgren, Jan Håfström, Olle Kåks and Ulla Wiggen, but the concept of creating a kind of art gallery has been aban-doned. In 1984, C F Reuterswärd's enamel paintings were inaugurated: the motifs run alongside the moving walkway as if they were accompany-ing the passengers being conveyed along the subway.

Ola Billgren, Ulla Wiggen, Olle Kåks and Jan Håfström did the paintings that originally decorated the pedestrian tunnel linking T-Centralen with the Järva line. All of them have now been withdrawn. Ola Billgren's paintings were portraits of Jesus typical of various ages. Passengers standing on the moving walkway were conveyed past a series of historical faces of Jesus, ending with a contemporary pop image.

*Paintings by Ulla Wiggen, Olle Kåks
and Ola Billgren.*

In the passage linking T-Centralen with the Järva line, Carl Fredrik Reuter-swärd's two enamel murals play with shapes as they emerge and are transformed. In 1984 these murals replaced a series of individual paintings by four artists (see previous spread).

In the vaulted chamber just before we descend into the platform area of the Järva line, P O Ultvedt has portrayed in silhouette the workers constructing the station and the scaffolding contraptions they used. Their shadowy figures surround us on all sides.

SLUSSEN

The Hökarängen – Slussen section was opened in October, 1950, and was the first section of the new underground to be finished. It was not until the mid-1960s, however, that the Slussen station was given any artistic treatment; this was an outcome of the public competition held in 1960, which led to the incorporation of art of various kinds and in various amounts at many stations.

In the ticket hall at the Hökens gata entrance, Aston Forsberg and Birger Forsberg made a non-figurative deep relief in light-coloured marble concrete entitled "Entrance Fee 70 öre", inaugurated in 1966. The same year, Sune Fogde decorated a wall in enamel and plaster, calling it "Upandown", in a pedestrian passage further into the station. The

Gun Gordillo: A sound dampening wall with artistic treatment using neon. View and detail.

Harald Lyth: "Derailed".

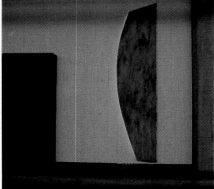

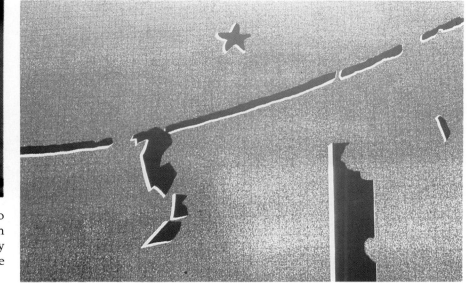

shaped plates are incorporated into the surface plaster of the wall in rhythmical patterns, and their shiny enamel surfaces contrast with the matt surface of the plaster.

Down on the platform, Aston Forsberg made a grill in iron and concrete between the two halves of the platform in 1964. In more recent years the rather shabby station area has been provided with so-called "loose pictures", similar in size to advertising posters.

Much later, in 1983, a glass painting by Harald Lyth was installed as a result of a closed competition. It has the difficult, not to say impossible, task of making the stained glass effective in two directions: inwards into the staff canteen, and outwards towards the general public in the ticket hall at Slussplan.

Sune Fogde: Upandown.

FARSTA CENTRUM

"I want to create warmth and a summery atmosphere out of what is basically cold and windy," is how Gunnar Larson explains his work of art entitled "Transformations in the Sky". Farsta Centrum is a surface station, and originally had no art work at all. At the turn of 1982—83, the high-roofed ticket hall was suffused with the chill of concrete until one day, a mass of ethereal acrylic paintings on shaped aluminium sheets was hung from the ceiling: coming in from the frosty cold outside was like entering a hanging garden.

In recent years, nearly all the new stations have been built north of Slussen. This has meant that art in the underground has not been evenly spread throughout the city, and people have complained. In response, Stockholm Transport and its Art Advisory Council have tried to ensure a more even distribution of art underground, and a number of old stations have been given an artistic face-lift.

BANDHAGEN

During the night of 21 September, 1983, a large sandstone rock from Öland was hoisted up on to the platform at Bandhagen station. Soon afterwards, a gigantic folding rule was fitted into place, parts of it resting low down near the ground, other parts twisting up and down like a worm on a fisherman's hook, forming carefully measured archways before eventually wrapping itself round the big, immovable stone. Finally, it bids farewell four metres up, outside the ticket hall. Or it could be the other way round—perhaps it is bidding "Good morning" outside the ticket hall entrance . . .

The Dane Freddy Fraek was the winner of the closed competition for the artistic design of Bandhagen station, which was designed by the architect Peter Celsing and opened without any works of art at all in November, 1954. Fraek's winning entry is a play on the contrast between what was created by nature, and a tool invented by man. Sometimes the scale is reduced, but sometimes it is enlarged, so that it can seem as if the train is suddenly changing speed—or perhaps it is just that we are all being jerked out of our normal way of thinking.

*Freddy Flaek's sculpture is a gigantic folding rule, which climbs over
a block of Öland stone and greets passengers at the entrance.
In 1987, the folding rule was clad in sheet copper with etched
and painted figures.*

RÅDMANSGATAN

Strindberg in a top hat, stiff shirt collar and an overcoat with a fur collar is what meets passengers rushing out of the exit leading to Tegnérgatan and, further up the hill, the author's last home: the flat known as the Blue Tower, now turned into a Strindberg Museum. He is staring straight at you, a serious expression on his face.

Behind him rage Inferno-like flames. The four enamel tiles making up the portrait meet at the tip of his nose and suddenly, just for a second, he looks like a meek, friendly old gentleman. But those sharp eyes of his soon bring you down to earth again.

The artist, Sture Valentin Nilsson, has lined up a series of linked pictures culminating in another portrait of Strindberg with tousled hair, melting into the Blue Tower which looms in the background. Just imagine standing in this underground passage and deciphering with difficulty Strindberg's handwriting, to discover the finest description we have of Stockholm in early spring!

Sture Valentin Nilsson has turned the station into a tribute to August Strindberg in the passage leading to the Strindberg Museum in the nearby Blue Tower.

ÖSTERMALMSTORG

In 1961, Siri Derkert won the open competition, which attracted 159 entries in all, with her "Gougings in Natural Concrete". The following year, at the age of 73, she descended into the cold, 36 metres below ground, to start on the strenuous task of transferring the ideas in the sketches on to the hard concrete. Using a sand-blasting technique developed by the Norwegian artist Carl Nesjar for his own work and for Picasso's large concrete sculptures, she created a continuous series of pictures on the 300-metre-long walls.

As in a strip cartoon, Siri Derkert uses sequence after sequence of images to comment on creative women, peace, the importance of playing and singing, men and children, and our duty to conserve our environment. Amidst the elegance of Östermalm are snatches of the International and the Marseillaise, their tunes linking the pictures together. "It is a sermon, and matters discussed in these sermons can never go out of date. They are: the Women's Movement, and Peace. I'm preaching these sermons here on the walls of the underground because City Hall and the walls of our churches are weighed down with the messages of past generations . . . The whole of history, as we know it, is a history of men by men. It is largely for that reason — for the unwritten history of women — that I decided to inscribe my concrete slabs in the Stockholm underground the way I did. The women's movement is the most important thing of all."

189

A sandblasting technique is used to scratch pictures onto the hard surface: light-coloured concrete is blasted to reveal dark stones underneath, or alternatively black concrete is blasted to uncover light stones. Playing, dancing and singing figures flit past among slogans, portraits of well-known women from the past, and an occasional man. This station was designed by Siri Derkert.

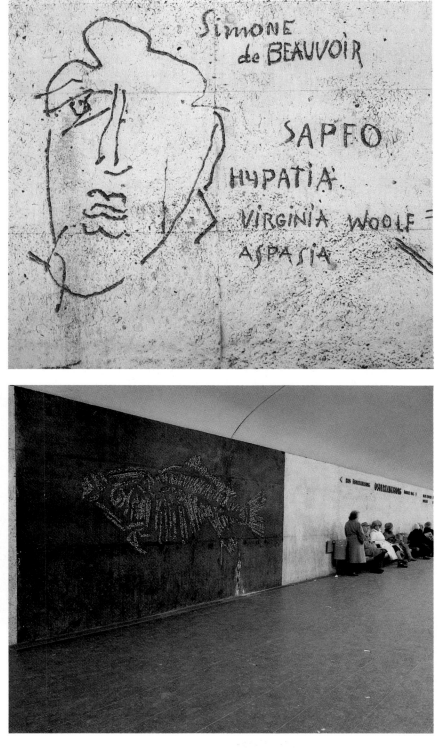

Simone de BEAUVOIR

SAPFO
HYPATIA
VIRGINIA WOOLF
ASPASIA

KARLAPLAN

Tor Hörlin's design in glazed stoneware was inaugurated in 1967. The tiles are arranged in a simple mosaic pattern in 16 areas dotted around the inside walls of the platform. In 1983 they were complemented by a photographic triptych, "That Day and that Sorrow", by Larseric Vänerlöf. The photographic montage is 96 metres long.

GÄRDET

An entomologist's dream: large, exotic beetles in shimmering colours, never seen before. Karl Axel Pehrson, artist and collector of insects, has conjured forth this dream in showcase after showcase. The beetles have been fashioned from remarkable materials, and have even been given Latin names of their own. Unfortunately, many of them have fallen prey to the collecting instincts of a different kind of collector: they have been stolen, and the showcases stand empty. Dreams can be difficult to recreate, and so no new beetle sculptures will be made.

Karl Axel Pehrson: Fantastic beetles.

MARIATORGET

The only entry in the 1961 competition to receive a prize in group II, "Mixture of advertising and artistic decoration", was "Stoneware", by the ceramist Karin Björquist and the architect Kjell Abramson. The original idea was that posters hung in this area would only advertise cultural events, but this was in fact only realized much later in the Kungsträdgården station.

The station was opened in May, 1964, and Asmund Arle's bronze sculpture "Person and Pillar" was also ready by then. It had won first prize in group IV, and the jury justified its decision thus: "By placing it next to the pillar, with the child turning towards it, the sculpture introduces a highly desirable sense of calm into this environment, which is so often full of hustle and bustle."

After winning a prize for them in the same competition, Britt-Louise Sundell duly constructed her wrought iron gates, "Domino", and in 1978–79 some more stoneware was supplied by Karin Björquist for the central platform area.

Around 1978, large so-called "brigade paintings" appeared—extempore graffiti with political overtones. Many of them were signed "Höken", and some years later Höken exhibited at one of Stockholm's art galleries, now using his own name.

Mariatorget station also has a number of so-called "loose pictures" on the walls alongside the track.

HORNSTULL

Together with Siri Derkert, Berndt Helleberg won first prize in the open competition judged in 1961. His work is called "Altamira".

The jury commented as follows: "A well thought-out entry with a feel for both the unity and the variation needed in the station. The sense of well-being induced by the background colour contrasts with the delicate, graceful decorations. The whole thing exudes warmth and cosiness, and makes those looking at it feel at home."

The dominant colour found in 20,000-year-old cave paintings is reproduced in the hand-made bricks covering the two long walls of the station. The brick is laid diagonally, and the artist has inset into its surface running and dancing shapes in black and white stone. They follow the track, meet the trains, disappear, then emerge once more like a melody.

The station, which was opened in 1964, is completely devoid of disturbing advertisements. An addition to the art work in the connecting tunnel was carried out in 1979.

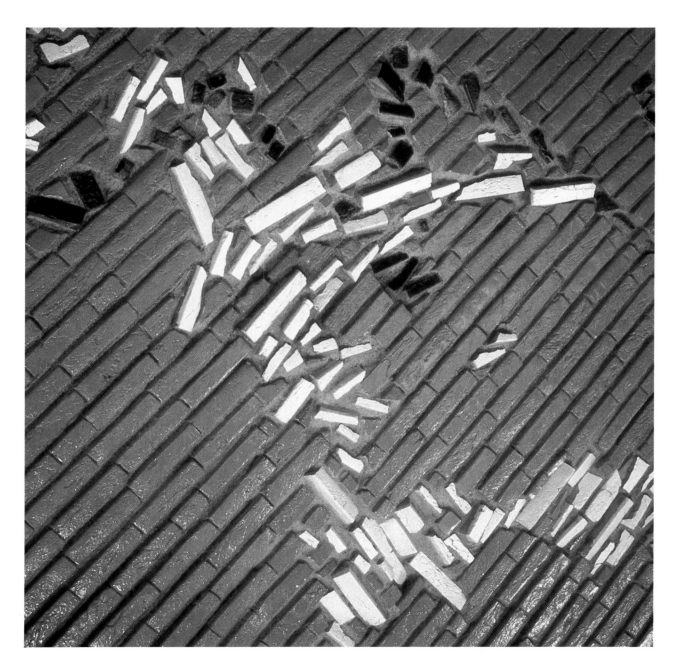

MIDSOMMARKRANSEN

The name of this station means "Midsummer Wreath", and students of the School of Arts, Crafts and Design combined with local residents to make a large midsummer wreath in painted wood. The station was decorated in time for Midsummer, 1979; it had been without any kind of art since its opening in April, 1964. A nearby wall was festooned with garlands, wreaths of flowers and photographs of the actual work on decorations taking place. There was also a plaque, with the following inscriptions: "Local residents made this midsummer wreath in the spring of 1979 at the community centre in Tegelbruksgatan near Lilla Torget. On 27 February, a full-scale model made of cardboard was hung in place to test the size and colours in their eventual context. Every flower and every leaf was cut and shaped from a piece of elder, then fitted onto a hoop made of pine. The paint was made from colour pigments, linseed oil, egg and water, and is known as egg oil tempera – an old, well-tried method. The decor was inaugurated on 21 June, 1979."

VÄSTERTORP

On one of the walls, a large air ballon seems to be drifting out of the station along the beautiful pedestrian tunnel designed by the AOS architectural office. In 1982, Jörgen Fogelquist created two murals on opposite walls, using sgraffito techniques, and called them "With the Eagle to the Pole". The street names in Väster- torp are often associated with snow, ice and winter, and the artist was in- spired to realize a long-cherished idea and use the two walls to depict Andrée's expedition to the North Pole by air balloon in 1897. The bal- loon's heavy drag lines leave trails along the white walls, and a blue band echoes the rhythm of the roof windows designed for the tunnel by the architects. A little further on, the pioneers' final camp is depicted, ex- actly as it was when found in 1930, with pieces of clothing, snow shoes, rifles and bits of skeletons scattered all around by the polar bears.

AXELSBERG

The AXELSBERG station has as many sculptures as there are letters in its name. They are about four metres high, in glass, iron, stone, concrete, sand, and plastic, some of them gilded, others untreated and rusty, and they form a line alongside the tracks towards a newly-built hotel for pensioners. The cave-like areas where each sculpture stands also act as sound insulation.

The sculptures are witty and poetic, and were made by four artists working in close cooperation: Leif Bolter, Veine Johansson, Inga Modén and Gösta Wessel.

Each letter represents a play on shapes on a sort of stage, separated from the next by concrete pillars at approximately 9-metre-intervals.

The back-cloth throughout is made up of rounded stones taken from sand-pits. The effect of scene-changes is achieved in that each shape stimulates a reaction until one realizes the letters form the name AXELSBERG.

The artists describe their work thus: "We wanted to achieve a restful rhythm, an extended space, a high level of sound absorption, and at the same time set up a witty play on the letters making up the name of the station; we aimed at arousing associations, thoughts and surprise.

MÄLARHÖJDEN

Margareta Carlstedt's long enamel paintings give the impression of an aquarelle, just finished and still wet. The sunny, ethereal archipelago atmosphere inspired the artist to create monumental pictures in a hard material which can stand rough treatment for many years. As if painted on many individual sheets of paper—the size of each tile was dictated by the enamelling oven—the two pictures extend in parallel for 145 metres underground.

"Ebb and Flow" won a prize in 1961. The jury commented: "The colours are fresh, rich in associations and richly varied. The whole thing gives a feeling of light and air."

Margareta Carlstedt adds: "The mural also contains music. A theme is developed and extends alongside the tracks, pianissimo, vibrato . . ."

MASMO

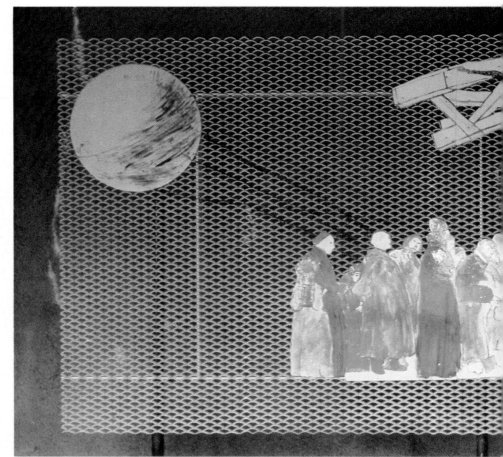

Masmo was the first of the so-called cave stations, with the original contours of the rock face very much visible despite being coated in a layer of sprayed concrete. This station was the architects' and engineers' prototype for a whole series of projected stations to be built to the north: Stadion, Tekniska Högskolan and the whole Järva line. The Masmo colour, a dark navy blue, was to be sprayed onto the concrete, and eventually an inner room of metal mesh constructed inside the cave so that passengers would be protected from what was then thought to be the negative impression created by the cave itself. Pictures could be mounted quickly and easily on the mesh alongside the tracks. The idea was that it would even be possible to unhook the various pictures in sections, and move them around the different stations.

Staffan Hallström, working together with Lasse Andréasson, made his "Bring the Sun into the Underground" in stoving enamelled sheet metal. "If you are working in caves, you must take account of the limitations imposed by the rock. Our strength was not that we were creating beautiful works of art, but that we were doing something new, introducing new ideas. Other artists reacted strongly to this concept of movable art, but we took the opposite view. We didn't really want to pave the way for a new type of underground art. We didn't want to create eternal monuments like Siri Derkert's Östermalmstorg station.

Of course her walls are good. But it's wrong that they should be just standing there, getting dirty, cracking, and growing ugly. No one dare touch them. We want it to be a living environment—not a church with eternal art. We are not interested in personal manifestations."

The station was finished in 1971, and opened on 10 January 1972. In 1964, the same two artists had created a 35-metre-long stoneware mural in T-Centralen, at the Sergels Torg exit. As a result of rebuilding works, part of the mural was dismantled and put in store, and what remains is only partly visible behind a kiosk selling season tickets. Presumably this contributed to the artists' positive attitude towards mobile art.

Carl Larsson's painting "The Entry of Gustav Vasa into Stockholm" plays a leading role in a suite of paintings on sheet metal. The artists Staffan Hallström and Lasse Andréasson have added to the picture. A group of people greet the king with a large sun on long strings: bring the sun down into the underground!

ALBY

"The experience of going down into the cave was overwhelming. The rock chambers were enormous. It was this experience which gave me inspiration. I was very irritated by the wire mesh, and should have tried to get it taken away from the roof." Olle Ängkvist turned Alby station into a "Secret Cave". A Phoenix rises from the ashes, flaming red and flapping its wings in pride; a labyrinth tempts onlookers to undertake bewildering explorations; a cult site with colourful little flowers in naive style spreads out and extends a flowery carpet over the walls and the arched roof of the cave. There are several sun symbols dotted about.

"Lower down, round the edges and underneath where the advertising posters were intended to go, I drew figures crying or playing naughty tricks, poking fun at advertisements. I did that spontaneously, while I was waiting. They weren't there in the sketches. Perhaps that's why there isn't any advertising in this station," suggests Olle Ängkvist.

STADION

The Stockholm Transport Art Advisory Council was founded in 1971, and the first stations it had anything to do with were Stadion and Tekniska Högskolan. The council did not manage to do away with the metal mesh, which had dominated the recently built station at Masmo. The mesh had already been ordered, and was intended for a whole series of stations. At least it was painted here, and this helped it to melt into the background of the marbled blue-green rock walls to some extent. There is no metal mesh on the short side walls and the centre arch, and Enno Hallek and Åke Pallarp seized the opportunity of showing what can be done in these underground caves. Indicating which direction to follow for locations on the surface, a letter S looking like a candy snake with an arrow for a head points to the sports complex known as Stadion, while the M standing for Musikhögskolan (College of Music) has grown feet and seems to be walking towards the correct exit. Olle Hjortzberg's famous old poster for the 1912 Olympic Games in Stockholm, with its fluttering banners and naked athletes, has been enlarged and placed on one of the short walls to provide an historical context and is an eye-catching greeting for passengers. The first thing one sees on the other side of the station is a large bench of thick planks with a back-rest covered in flowers, and the connecting passage has a colourful rainbow of hope, giving the rocky arch a sense of libera-

Enno Hallek: Direction indicator and bench.

Wooden decorations might be an inviting bench where you can rest a while, or a direction indicator pointing to the College of Music or Stadium exits. Enno Hallek and Åke Pallarp did the painting.

tion as it braces itself to bear the weight pressing down from above. The dominant light colour and the soft, humorous, wooden features in bright colours give the whole cave a carefree sense of freedom.

The Stadion and Tekniska Högskolan stations were opened in September, 1973, and received a spontaneous and enthusiastic reception from the general public. That reception was important for the trend towards more open caves in future stations.

TEKNISKA HÖGSKOLAN

It is easy to see that Lennart Mörk, the artist responsible for Tekniska Högskolan, is an experienced stage designer. The station is painted the same colour as soil, the life-giving Mother Earth, and against this background are a series of details from the world of technology—Tekniska Högskolan means "College of Technology". The station is designed as a concentrated lesson in the way the laws of nature have been perceived down the centuries, from Plato to Copernicus, Kepler, Descartes, Polhem, Maxwell, Einstein and so on. Focal points, orientation indicators in each of the four corners of the station, are large, painted polyhedra. They are symbols of Plato's view of the four elements: the octahedron stands for air, the tetrahedron for fire, the six-sided cube for the earth, and the twenty-sided icosahedron for water. Their projections are marked on the dark floor in the form of thin, inlaid lines. The ether, the universe, is symbolized by a dodecahedron, a twelve-sided glass case hanging from the vaulted main ceiling. Here is the black hole of the universe. In two places, the artist forces the metal mesh on the ceiling above our heads out of the way. At one of them, the orange-coloured wing of Icarus bursts through the mesh. On the other side, Newton's apple falls through the roof, illustrating the law of gravity but also evoking the scent of a real apple in the world above ground.

Lennart Mörk has turned this station into a scenographic depiction of the history of technology. Here and there is a portrait of a human being.

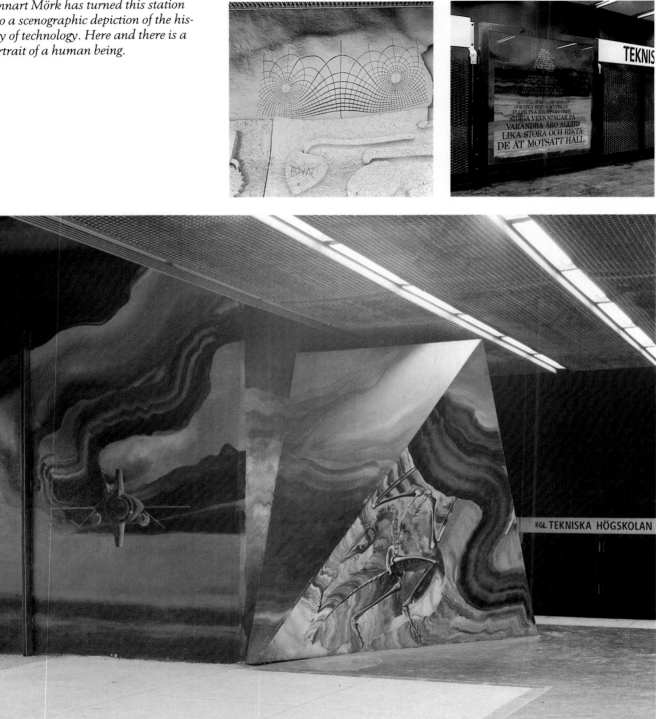

Newton's falling apple and Daedalus's wing plunging earthwards.

The way Lennart Mörk designs details to integrate into the chamber as a whole, is masterful: there is no question of individual bits being added together, as at Stadion.

UNIVERSITETET

The Alby and Universitetet stations were built at the same time, and opened in January, 1975. Both had empty walls for painting on. As we come down the escalator at Universitetet, we enter a sort of pergola or leafy chamber. At the south end is a green, summery landscape, and at the north end an evocation of autumn with rustling yellow leaves. In between, pines and fir trees loom up in a rocky landscape. The artist, Pär Andersson, created a painted garden and seasonal landscapes as a link with the Bergianska Gardens not far away on the surface. The College of Forestry used to be located here as well.

BERGSHAMRA

The theme of this station is "Voices from the Past", and it is designed as a symphony of words and pictures from some 300 million years ago to the present day. Göran Dahl treated his task as a huge collage, using images from various periods and a variety of techniques, with the result that the perspective moves forward through time until it reaches the present, our day. The floor is used quite a lot for pictures, such as coelacanths like layers in fossil organisms, illustrating the development process of life. The coelacanths developed into the animals which gradually emerged from the water to become four-legged land-dwellers. The trains rush by, just as the images rush by through time: the skeleton of an ancient bird, a frog, then a leap straight on to the oldest known runic inscription from Kylver on Gotland. After 1,500 years, its message is still mysterious but beautiful from a calligraphic point of view. Nearby is a reproduction of the Rökstenen from Östergötland. The longest continuous runic inscription in existence was originally made in the 9th century, and here, it is blasted on to polished grey granite.

A revolutionary Russian train of culture from the early 1920s, with the slogan "Long live the proletarian world-revolution", has now acquired a successor in the form of Carl Johan De Geer's painting depicting a book bus which he actually did decorate in 1968 for journeys through the north of Sweden. In the middle of all the pictures, as if keeping them in order, is an enlarged photograph of a man standing on a roof-top, conducting a concert of factory whistles in Leningrad around 1920.

Carl Johan De Geer: Book bus.

Kristina Anshelm: Russian train of culture.

Göran Dahl: Enamel painting "Chaplin Tatlin".

Göran Dahl made the big collage assisted by Thomas Theander and Larseric Vänerlöf.

Using sandblasting techniques, Göran Dahl reproduced the runic inscriptions from the Rökstenen onto polished granite slabs; frogs jump and fish swim in the terrazzo floor, and on the adjacent wall is a gleaming red bicycle on the bright glass surface.

Göran Dahl: My daughter's bicycle.

DANDERYDS SJUKHUS

Pierre Olofsson: The tree of life.

This station takes its name from the hospital it serves. Hertha Hillfon has scratched the names of ancient medicines and herbs on shimmering gold plates of clay, which are immured in the passageway leading to the hospital. Here and there are pictures of plants, and a dove flies among the herbs: yarrow, elegant mint, hyssop, motherwort, camomile, elder, dandelion, rosemary, basil, mint . . . What marvellous names, full of poetry and fragrance, to distract our minds from the stress of modern life which forces us to become hustling automata! The mysterious female head on a pillar, her hair glittering with gold, gazes at the serpent symbolizing the art of medicine, many metres long, twisting and turning to form a sign of eternity.

This station, home of the serpent and herb garden, was opened in January, 1978. A little later, in 1980, Pierre Olofsson created a mural at the southern exit on the theme ''The Tree of Life''.

221

MÖRBY CENTRUM

Karin Ek's and Gösta Wessel's station looks like a fluffy dessert with whipped cream and ice cream in pastel colours and a coating of thinned caramel. As a result of the shadow painting technique, the station seems all pink and white from one side, but all light grey-blue and white from the other. At the bottom of the escalator is a corrugated sheet-iron wall painted in the same way.

"We got the idea for our design from the special characteristics of the rock face, which we tried to exploit.

We placed the main emphasis on creating an integrated environment, and the movement of the passengers is an important factor in how they see it all. The contours of the rock face on the walls and the roof were painted in such a way that one's impression of the colours varies according to the view-point. The shape of the areas painted in a given colour are the same as they would be if we had placed a powerful spotlight at one end of the platform and painted in the shadows cast by the rock face.

The pictures in the showcases show various methods used when working underground with rock. These methods change, and what seems to us contemporary will be seen in quite a different light only a few decades hence. Our work and that of the workers who constructed the underground is over—but the station will change as time goes by and as the people who use it also change. They will continue the story."

KUNGSTRÄDGÅRDEN

A pink copy of a half-naked war-god at the older entrance watches over this underground chamber, the City terminus of the Järva line. This god of war originally stood on the roof of Rådhuset, the Town Hall. Now it belongs to Stadsmuseet, like many other originals used as models by Ulrik Samuelson in creating his work.

Most of the rock face is bare in this station, the blasting scars are visible all over the walls, so are the boreholes, and the water trickling from invisible cracks in the bedrock 36 metres under the surface is left to find its own way down the walls until it reaches a narrow gutter between the wall and the floor. The soft, fluffy, green algae spread over the hard surface in varying shapes and forms. To be on the safe side, the roof is reinforced and covered in a layer of sprayed concrete in a dull moss-green colour. A rope painted in various colours marks the joining between the sprayed concrete and the bare rock walls. Here and there, fixed on to cast pedestals, a yellow or orange mask, grinning or grimacing, grows out of the rock. These masks, and also a male and female torso, are made from casts of sculptural details from the Makalös Palace, built in the 17th century as a private residence of the De la Gardie family and later used as a theatre until it burned down in 1825. It was situated above where the Kungsträdgården underground station now lies, and one of the showcases there has a picture of the palace.

Thin lines marked on the sprayed concrete in the roof show where the streets are on the surface, the location of Molin's fountain, and where the famous elm trees are in Kungsträdgården. To remind us all of what can be done when people unite to take action, as they did when they prevented the elms from being felled, a piece of an elm trunk—cast in stone — reminds us that we must not allow ourselves to become apathetic. The spontaneous efforts of the general public, culimating in the so-called "Battle of the elms", forced local politicians to adopt a new approach to questions of town planning. A stone garden and a stone waterfall, with a little water trickling slowly over the barock stone shapes, is an underground reflection of the Kungsträdgården and its dazzling fountains up above. This station is full of hints and associations. Large sections of a harlequin's costume billow up in the roof near the escalator and remind passengers of the theatres on the surface: part of the material has turned inside out, and is the colour of a summer sky. Everything is festive and frenzied, or was a moment ago. A length of cord or rope, a curtain, mooring poles for Venetian gondolas now out of sight, a large-size ringpull from a beer can inlaid in the terrazzo floor—all these things indicate there has just been a party here, the tell-tale signs are still around. Speaking figuratively, death has also entered the stage.

Cultural posters in the pedestrian passage.

Artistic planning for this station started early, in the middle of 1974, over three years before work on it finished. This early start and the concentrated efforts of the artist, the architect, engineers and the Working Party of the Stockholm Transport Art Advisory Council have resulted in an integrated artistic design for the environment, something which is unfortunately very rare nowadays when new buildings are constructed.

Much later, in January 1987, a new entrance to this station was opened. Passengers leaving the trains emerge in Arsenalsgatan, right in the city centre, amidst the imposing financial houses and cultural institutions for music, the theatre, art and architecture. Deep down in the primary rock, the artist playfully rolls out his chequered carpet to form a terrazzo path over a footbridge across what could be an archaeological excavation: frag-

ments of stone from old buildings, balustrades, old lanterns in *art nouveau* style and modern neon strip-lights twinkling away in the darkness, rocks, an old cooking range in green marble with water-lilies painted on a pitch-black background where the fire should be, masks, bits of broken stone columns . . . From its elevated position overlooking it all with a gaze of eternal serenity, a mask opens its mouth and water gushes forth, tum-

Kungsträdgården station is one of the finest contemporary examples of how close cooperation between artist, architect, engineers and the Stockholm Transport Art Advisory Council has succeeded in creating an integrated artistic whole out of a subterranean cave whose primary function is to facilitate the transportation of passengers.

bling from one hollowed-out stone to another and eventually watering the living moss, ferns and ivy growing at the bottom of the moat. Watching over both scenes from each side of the opening leading into the station itself are the muse of architecture with her set-square and the muse of painting with her palette. The light-blue of the reinforced concrete sky smiles constantly upon these subterranean scenes. Straight ahead is a gruesome-looking Hercules with a lion's mane painted in the same colours as the original of which this is a copy. Bobbing up and down on the floor is a blue and yellow oil-drum, and a black streak across the pattern of the terrazzo floor suggests devasting oil pollution. Ulrik Samuelson has polished part of the primary rock itself and fashioned on its surface a gilded cross in deep relief. It glows magically against the solid, silent mass of rock, and suggests how cave chambers of the future might develop: sculptures could be made in the primary rock itself. The artist and everyone else involved have spared no effort so that passengers can enjoy the most beautiful settings of all in the thirty-year history of art in the underground.

This station contains many castings from architectural features borrowed from various times and various buildings, including the Makalös Palace. Ulrik Samuelson was the artistic director.

RÅDHUSET

The station is salmon pink throughout, rather like a dressing-room table drawer full of glamorous underwear from the 1940s. However, the man responsible, Sigvard Olsson, claims it is the same shade as can be found in the Atlas Mountains, furthest in. When the artist submitted his proposals for Rådhuset station in sketch form, they consisted of a powder compact, four A-4 pages of text and three colour samples. Not a particularly auspicious beginning for what turned out to be one of the most stylish stations on the whole Järva line. The rock chamber has been designed to give the impression of an excavation, where bits and pieces from earlier times have become visible as the work proceeded.

Sigvard Olsson says of his station: "When people started digging to make way for the underground, they gradually worked their way through layers with remains from previous ages. Of course, they took away as much as they needed to take in order to do the job, but here and there a few fragments would emerge and be left in place, whether it be for reasons of convenience or just laziness. That's why they found the base of Bolinder's (or is it Separator's) enormous chimney here at one end of the platform, and at the other a petrified wood-pile from some period of crisis. A few straw mats are still sticking out of one of the walls, and in a pedestrian tunnel they uncovered an old store of root vegetables. By an amazing stroke of luck,

232

Baskets for storing root vegetables.

the tunnel exit happened to coincide with a richly decorated 17th century gateway, through which north-bound trains pass just as they enter the station.

"The remarkable thing is that all these remains, recent ones as well as ancient ones, have taken on the same pinkish colour, the same melancholy shade which, incidently, you also find in the Atlas Mountains, furthest in. It was difficult to produce this pink colour, it is a sensitive shade and has to be exact. Countless vain attempts were made, and in the end I was forced to go to Norway and mix it in a garage outside Oslo.

"The pink walls are not so sensitive to damp stains and lime deposits, nor are they so vulnerable to defacement. I have assumed from the start that they will be defaced and scribbled on. Everybody leaves traces behind, and this is in keeping with my idea. It is an excavated rock chamber with fragments from earlier ages, into which people have inserted new technical contraptions such as lifts, escalators and pipes, painted in shiny bright colours.

"Incidentally, I don't understand what is wrong with caves. When they're on holiday, some people travel for miles in order to go and look at caves. They are exciting places with stalactites and things, and traces of prehistoric times.

I think the underground is much slandered. It's time somebody did something about it."

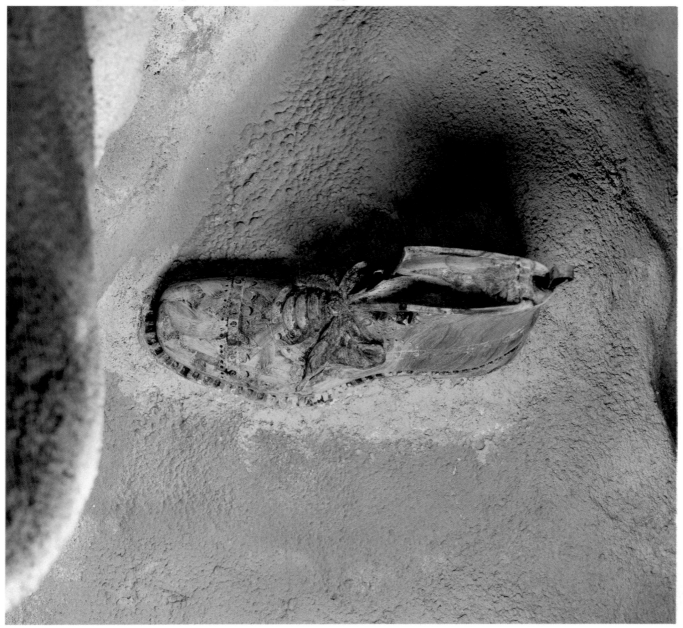

"The Goloshes of Fortune", a sign from a shoeshop in Fleminggatan.

FRIDHEMSPLAN

The old line to Hässelby and the new Järva line meet at Fridhemsplan. The old part of the station has no art work, whereas the new part has been turned into a sea station by Ingegerd Möller. The walls and roof of the cave are stippled, as if the waves of the sea were constantly whipping up a spray. A large showcase in the centre of the station contains a genuine boat from Blekinge, with a brownish-red sail. Up in the arched roof a large sea-bird by Torsten Renqvist is soaring with broad, white,

Torsten Renquist: Albatross

outstretched wings. It is constructed from wood, and the joinings clearly show how all the individual bits were pieced together, until the bird's wingspan reached three metres.

Along the platform, Ingegerd Möller has lined up a number of showcases, like display windows, exhibiting a stretch of beach over a period of 15 years. The first one is dominated by natural materials, but plastic gradually takes over, all kinds of rubbish creeps in, and in the last one, the beach is covered in oil.

STADSHAGEN

Lasse Lindqvist has played with the concept of footballers chasing over the green surface of the grassy pitch by painting his picture onto a corrugated sheet so that if you look at it from an angle to the right or left, you see a different picture, while these pictures merge when seen from in front, and thus the illusion of movement is created.

The original pictures of footballers have been added to over the years, and there are now similar pictures featuring other sports, and also flags fluttering on the corrugated metal, indicating which direction the trains go.

VÄSTRA SKOGEN

This station is named after Västra skogen, "Western Forest", also known as Ingentingskogen, "Nothing Forest", the forest that doesn't exist: there is a small bit of it left near the station. Both the place and the names are shrouded in mystery and myth.

Sivert Lindblom decided to preserve this feature in his design for the unusually large station. It is as dark as the primary rock behind the sprayed concrete, mysterious, and not a little uncanny. Here and there is a burst of colour in the form of regular rectangles or irregularly shaped, tiled sur-

faces, usually standing free in front of the walls. They are either closed shapes, or they give the impression of rushing forwards. Sometimes the pattern is such that it is reminiscent of the embroidered edges of old cushions, enlarged and billowing out into the station. The colours follow set patterns, and there is a touch of oriental atmosphere over the whole thing. Ulrik Samuelson helped with the ceramic tiles. Shapes sink down from the roof (or perhaps they are climbing up to it?), their heads turned round their own profile, that

of the artist. The same idea recurs in the long profile-sculpture opposite the escalator, which has twelve thin white vertical lines down it.

Sivert Lindblom comments: "In the old days, artists had certain norms to work by, they provided the absolute starting point. In every period there were principles one observed. Nowadays, nothing is given. We have no ornament we can call that of our own time, instead we can pick and choose at will from earlier periods of other countries, everything can be approached in a spirit of

"I've used the profile motif before, and it was fun to do it again. It's made from the same material as the floors and plinths, and just grows out of the existing architecture."

uninhibited improvisation. I want to set myself a certain working method, as a voluntary restriction. The most severe and binding principles provide more than enough space, freedom and excitement.

"Working like this is like playing chess. No other game is so bound by rules, yet no other game gives so much scope for completely new and unexpected solutions."

"I thought it would be interesting to use ceramic tiles again. A colour sequence is fixed for each picture, which is then reproduced in various directions and directional systems. The tiles running along the plinths link the bigger tile pictures together, as if they were all dancing on the same tightrope."

Large shapes in ceramic tiles stand out against the dark sprayed-concrete wall; some of them seem to be moving, indicating a direction, while others are still, as if resting. Sivert Lindblom uses a thin, blue continuous line to indicate that trains are going northwards, and a yellow line on the platform for southbound trains.

SOLNA CENTRUM

Going by underground is a great adventure, full of contrasts. Quite unlike Västra Skogen, the station at Solna greets passengers with a blazing cadmium-red sky and nearly a thousand metres of green fir forest painted on to the sprayed concrete. Here and there are clearings in the forest, little stories in pictures or sculpted in little windows reminiscent of a peep-show.

Anders Åberg and Karl-Olov Björk cooperated on this station.

"The times they are a-changing", sings Bob Dylan in one of the peep-shows, among the little summer cottages with picturesque names like Pine Tops, Happy Cottage, Sunny Smiles, Sunshine Lodge . . . and on the little hill just behind them is the stiff, white mansion looking suspiciously like the White House. In the background is the outline of a procession of demonstrators painted on the inner wall of the box. On the red walls there is no sign of the mean houses and tower blocks of Hagalund, but instead we find mainly the deserted villages of the far North and removal vans heading southwards, derelict community centres, bare hills where there used to be forests, aeroplanes spraying not only trees but also angry berry-pickers, elks, a powerful Ardennes carthorse dragging lumber behind it, the local bread van on the winding roads, factory complexes, deserted houses with delightfully carved verandas . . . Hints of romanticism and nostalgia mingle with the biting criticism.

There are a lot of elks portrayed in public art nowadays. At Solna station, elks are both painted and sculpted against the red sunset of the sprayed concrete. In picture after picture, Anders Åberg and Karl-Olov Björk depict nature, environmental pollution, rural depopulation, music . . .

The two artists comment on their work as follows: "There is an enormous interest in clear, comprehensible, perhaps even humorous pictures. People have to recognize that this art business is not just for a tiny elite. We're doing something for all those people who've footed the bill for our training through their taxes. The moral question is important. There's something perverted about just sitting at a drawing board and letting the manual workers do the actual work. You've got to be able to work with your hands yourself, or else you risk losing contact with a large section of society. The social isolation of the artist and the spirit of competition result in a kind of neuroticism. It's difficult to work together . . . The fact that we have cooperated on this makes us feel enormously optimistic about the future . . . It feels like the beginning of something that will go on, it clarifies things, points the way."

247

NÄCKROSEN

"A waterlily day winding brooklets and roads
a waterlily joy
A mist
A haze over the trees
and farms and hamlets wait for the dusk"

The name of this station means "waterlily", and it is marvellous to stand here, more than twenty metres down into the primary rock, reading a poem by Gunnar Björling full of concentrated visions of eternity, inscribed on the floor at my feet; close by is a group of large stones giving the feel of being on a lake shore, and up above my head a lake covered with waterlilies in flower. This is what can happen in Lizzie Olsson-Arle's station, designed as a huge collage of texts, stones, bits of old tiled stoves, glazed tiles from the Strindberg house at Karlaplan (how could they pull it down?), film props, photos . . . Memories of Filmstaden, the film studio complex that used to be located nearby, suggest the history of film-making by mentioning the first and last films to be made here—"Körkarlen" (The Driver—Selma Lagerlöf's novel on which it was based was translated into English as *Thy Soul Shall Bear Witness!*), directed by Victor Sjöström in 1920, and "En passion" (A Passion), written and directed by Ingmar Bergman in 1968. Little Johannes, eight years old, wrote on the floor: "Please take care of the hedgehog."
The station was opened in 1975.

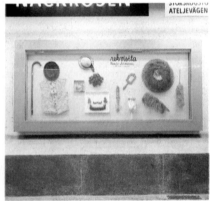

HALLONBERGEN

A white cave filled with enlarged children's drawings on the walls, and something similar in the form of sculptures in the arches between the tracks. The very name Hallonbergen, which means ''Raspberry Mountains'', evokes fairy tales, summer, play, plays on words and the spelling of words. Elis Eriksson, who had previously created a marvellous strip cartoon about a character called Pavan, and Gösta Wallmark have made a station suitable for children of all ages. The various fittings are coloured shocking pink, suggesting cream cakes.

Gösta Wallmark: ''I used my own childhood drawings, which my mother had saved. I also included what my own children have drawn. The hopscotch frame is an exact copy of one in a schoolyard, with mistakes and all.''

Elis Eriksson: ''It was a marvellous idea, using children's drawings. Gösta and I wanted to agree on an idea, all this is really beyond both of us. We didn't think our artistic ideas were good enough: it's much better to borrow somebody else's material, as we have done here. Besides, if anyone complains about anything, we can always refer them to Anna, aged 11, for instance—'You think this is awful? Oh, what a pity! But it's nothing to do with me—it was Anna who drew it like that. Next time I see her I'll tell her you thought she had made a real mess of it.' ''

Elis Eriksson and Gösta Wallmark were inspired by children's drawings and scribblings to reproduce them in sculptures and as paintings on the white sprayed concrete walls and roof.

KISTA

Lars Erik Falk's 16-metre-high sculpture zooms up from ground level, through the roof, and up into the air. It is made of painted aluminium girders, fixed at an angle of 73°. It introduces a sense of liveliness, adds vigour and excitement. Moreover, it is in fascinating contrast to the art work in other nearby stations, introducing a harder, cleaner tone. The colour scheme for the whole station was chosen by the artist, and he used colour to focus our attention even more on the sculpture in its architectural context. The sculpture is painted in such a way that the morning travellers taking trains to the city centre see its red and orange side, while those on the way home see its soothing blue and green side.

HUSBY

Birgit Broms' station is an early summer cave, as green as newly opened leaves. The first thing one sees on the platform here is a long line of pictures with archipelago motifs, 27 metres under the surface of the earth. The old archipelago boats chug away in procession past rows of tree trunks. We can see the steamship Waxholm, also Sandhamns Express, Norrskär . . . All of them are on their way out to ply the sunny archipelago.

AKALLA

Right out at the end of one of the Järva line's branches is the Akalla station, a yellow cave with large stoneware pictures by Birgit Ståhl-Nyberg. It was opened in 1977. The station contains a shelter, and the artist chose its smooth walls for her six concentrated pictures on various themes, leaving the sprayed concrete untouched apart from being painted in one colour. The stoneware, fired at almost 1,300°, is a hard, durable material with a shiny surface which repels dust. The forms are strictly constructed with the spirit of Fernand Léger, that master of modern monumental art, hovering in the background. One depicts various ideal images of men in a line of development from left to right. Superman draws his pistol, a footballer guards his goal, a bureaucrat rushes along, a building worker plies his trade, and furthest to the right is a rare phenomenon in the history of art, a father carrying a child.

The ideal woman is portrayed in the form of a woman gradually shaking off her oppressed role in which she is occupied with and trapped by her image as a pretty object of desire. At the far right, she has become a liberated woman distributing leaflets: "United we are strong".

The last picture concentrates on a man's working day, showing the harrassed, efficient, brief-case-carrying executive using his elbows effectively as usual in order to get on.

The stoneware walls offer a contrast to the rest of the Järva line.

Birgit Ståhl-Nyberg: Detail for stoneware relief depicting various male ideals. The whole picture is reproduced on the next page.

Two of Birgit Ståhl-Nyberg's six pictures are opposite each other
and depict various ideal men and women respectively.

HUVUDSTA

Per Holmberg's inspiration for this station was Semiramis' hanging gardens of Babylon. The driving force behind it is the sheer joy of adornment and decoration, of making that extra effort to cheer us up and give us stimulating experiences. Vegetation in the form of wire mesh hangs from the ceiling like veils, and the floor has been made into one big espalier in brilliant neon-pink, red, yellow . . . The colours of the lattice-work slats go in pairs, one colour increases while the other reduces and gives way to a new colour, and the pattern continues thus like a wave, giving an illusion that the espalier is three-dimensional and releasing itself from the floor. The wave pattern on the cable box works similarly, the basic colours emerging, increasing and eventually disappearing in pulsating fashion. Running up the walls are decorative bands taken from the cross-vaulting of old Roslagen churches, seemingly measuring the rough surface of the sprayed concrete in zig-zag movements. The large tube in the roof, which is there to conceal pipes and cables and to reduce the noise, is decorated with a green spiral band which concentrates and increases its speed of forward movement every time it comes to one of the supporting poles—a twining creeper in the "Hanging Gardens".

VRETEN

"Sky of Cubes" was the title of Takashi Naraha's prizewinning entry in the 1978 competition. The station, completed in 1985, realizes the artist's intentions on the whole, but unfortunately, for various reasons it was not possible to have cubes on the floor. But they hover under the roof and on the walls of this grey cave, cubes in various sizes depicting pieces of sky and light clouds. A cube of sky, a sky of cubes. Takashi Naraha moved from Japan to the Göinge area in Sweden about ten years ago for the sake of the black stone diabase, and often works with contrasts. This dark cave 30 metres under ground has lots of cubes depicting patches of summery sky on the roof and walls, shiny ones on the roof and matt ones on the walls. At the entrance to the station is a shiny, polished cube of black stone. As black as night, it stands there on its point slightly askew, and greets us as we embark on our journey under ground.

SUNDBYBERGS CENTRUM

Lars Kleen designed the station as a tribute to various aspects of craftsmanship in the building trade. Peter Tillberg and Michael Söderlundh contributed the paintings. Kleen constructed a series of house façades from old Sundbyberg, showing off the art of tiling, a stone façade, a bowed brick wall, etc. A complicated roof projects from the platform floor, and the impressive skills of the tinsmith have turned the lines of the joints and the bow-shaped contours into a magnificent piece of sculpture. The craft of the stone mason is displayed in a granite façade, its massive presence reaching out and impressing us just as we are dwarfed by the sheer weight of a stone-built house. A brick wall, actually made of wood, extends in waves and draws our attention to a remarkable corner; the form of the house forces itself on our attention, and it is impossible to walk past unheeding. There is a sense of incorruptibility, of an overwhelming desire to pass on a message, to make us appreciate and safeguard vanishing values. It is a place to visit and to derive inspiring strength from, this station dedicated to thousands and thousands of people.

"I have tried to give everything it is in an artist's power to give in this station. There is no better way of doing that than by turning an underground station into a work of art."

Peter Tillberg: "Hovering Rocks", and Michael Söderlundh: "Parkland".

265

Lars Kleen: "Bazaar". Wooden building from Sundbyberg at the turn of the century.

"The Window Opposite". Free version of a Sundbyberg painting by Peter Tillberg, 1970.

"Arla". From a Sundbyberg house demolished about 1930.

Michael Söderlundh: Silhouette painting in terrazzo.

DUVBO

Gösta Sillen's starting point for his "Cave" was the thought that once you start digging into rock, you never know what you might find: pictures, fragments of things, various experiences. What we eventually see is what emerges after blasting has taken place and the masses of loose stone removed. The further you penetrate into the rock, the more you find, layer upon layer. Sometimes, everything is revealed: a polished slab with bits of forgotten peel, sheets of newspaper with text almost completely obliterated, fossils . . . Traces, our own traces.

The design of this station displays a degree of honesty which one has to admire: the artist has made no attempt to turn the cave into anything but what it is—a cave. Light plays tantalizingly on the various objects in the walls waiting to be discovered, and we can make discoveries ourselves while we are waiting for our train, or dashing quickly along the platform. But not all the stations can be presented as the caves they actually are! That would just be boring. The big attraction of this array of stations is that they vary so much in their mode of expression.

RISSNE

Walking along a white floor and feeling as if the law of gravity no longer applies is a remarkable experience deep down underground. All the while, time runs along the walls, playing tag. Using simple means, Madeleine Dranger and Rolf H Reimers have managed to create a cheerful, light and stimulating station in pastel shades, with a blue line along the edge of the platform and a projection of the escalator area like an arch on the ground coming towards you.

The station is designed like an axis of time. Many a useful history lesson can be learned by reading the long lines of text up to fifty deep along one of the long walls in this cave station, which is like a wedge driven into the hard, black primary rock. An occasional relief in among the text creates rhythm and a pause in the mass of words. On the opposite wall are maps corresponding to the text. Colour codes help to classify the wealth of information—religion has yellow text, technology is blue, culture blue-pink, politics green, and everyday events red. The cave has become a veritable sea of poetic views on history.

The artist has called the station, which was opened in 1985, "See you in the 15th Century"; at the sketch stage in 1978, the intended title was to be "Once Upon a Time".

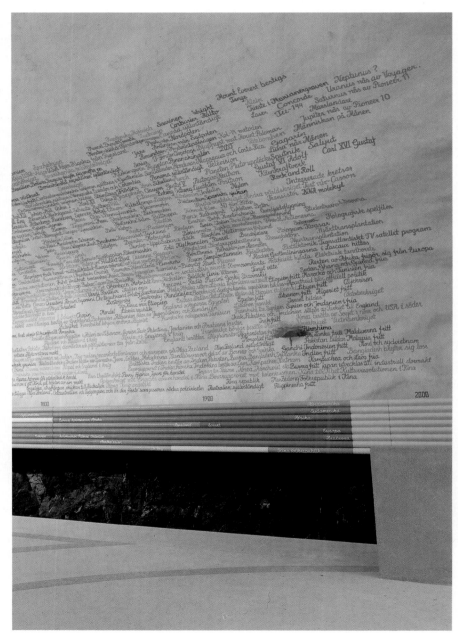

RINKEBY

Nils Zetterberg pretends that this station is a cave full of prehistoric finds. Pictures using various techniques and differing in character are held together by the brick-red colour of the background. Tiny little objects found in the area at the excavation stage have been blown up to large mosaics glittering with gold. A Roslagen rose hangs from the roof, its petals looking like the blades of oars and radiating outwards like beams of the sun to remind us of sea journeys undertaken in former times. In amongst all this are runic inscriptions and flying birds, racing alongside the blue trains as they come thundering into the station.

Roslagen rose hanging from the roof by Sven Sahlberg.
Bird pictures by Lennart Gram.

TENSTA

Helga Henschen has designed the Tensta station at Järvafältet as a tribute to the unfortunate residents who have to live in this concrete jungle of a suburb. Many of them are immigrants.

The background colour of this station is white, as at the two neighbouring stations, Näckrosen and Hallonbergen; with their different poetic effects, they are shining pearls on this long necklace of underground caves. At Tensta, we find a green forest of fir trees, painted with a fine brush using shadowing techniques, prehistoric animals, and sculpted birds in long rows on shelves formed by the rock face. When the train has left and exposed the wall on the other side, we find a quotation from Hans Palmstierna: "We must build a world fit to live in, fit for us and also for future generations."

The floor is covered in stars, trees and fir needles engraved into the terrazzo.

The wall surfaces are covered in pictures and a lot of text, quotations, written in clear, somewhat naive schoolboy style: "The world has come to Sweden: we have a unique opportunity of enriching our culture, of making our lives more interesting through contact with immigrants." (Birger Norman) "No, do not allow yourself to be used, but use your time well; no, never let yourself be cowed—you support us, we'll support you, we breathe life into one another." (Wolf Biermann.)

Helga Henschen has covered the uneven surface of the sprayed concrete with paintings, sculptures and texts obviously related to graffiti in character. There are also pictures in the floor.

HJULSTA

Right at the end of one branch of the Järva line, art under ground has taken on the form of an art exhibition. Small individual pictures are hung with no consideration given to the context. This way of working is in complete contrast to that adopted at the terminus in the inner city, Kungsträdgården.

Seven artists are represented in the station. In addition to those whose pictures are reproduced here, they are: Magnus Rimling, Olle Magnusson, Ruth Rydfelt, Birgitta Karlsson and Ove Thorsén.

Acrylic painting on plastic paper by Eva Nyberg: "It's Up To Us".

Christina Rundqvist-Andersson: "Birds".

Overview of stations with artistic decoration

STATION	ARTIST	YEAR	SKETCH	DECORATION
AKALLA (p 257–259)	Birgit Ståhl-Nyberg 1928–1982	1977	1975	Cave in ochre. Ceramic pictures on the platform wall, depicting ideal images of men and women, everyday tasks, dance and work.
ALBY (p 204–205)	Olle Ängkvist born 1922	1975	1973	Decorations—figures and symbols in various colours against a green background.
ASPUDDEN (p 169)	P G Thelander born 1936	1987	1982 personal commission	Penguin sculpture, roof paintings, enamel reliefs on the track walls.
AXELSBERG (p 200)	Leif Bolter born 1941 Veine Johansson born 1941 Inga Modén born 1947 Gösta Wessel born 1944	1983	1980	Sculptured variations on the station name. Each letter is a free-standing sculpture, 3–4 m high, in glass, concrete, sand and iron. Originally a project from a further education course at the College of Art.
BANDHAGEN (p 184–185)	Freddy Fraek born 1935	1983 1987	1982	Sculpture in the form of a gigantic folding rule. Clad in sheet copper.
BERGSHAMRA (p 216–219)	Göran Dahl born 1944 Carl Johan De Geer born 1938 Kristina Anshelm born 1942	1978	1974	The history of evolution in pictures on 66 sheets of glass, 2.2 × 1.5 m, and 2 pictures 2.5 × 8 m. Runes on granite wall. Photography undertaken partly in cooperation with Gunnar Dahl, Tomas Theander and Larseric Vänerlöf.
	Göran Dahl	1987	1985	Supplement at southern exit.

Aspudden. P G Thelander: Penguin for the station.　　　*Bredäng.*

STATION	ARTIST	YEAR	SKETCH	DECORATION
BLACKEBERG	Ruben Heleander born 1931	1987	1984 work creation scheme	Naturalistic painting on clinker attached to the track wall.
BREDÄNG	Lena Kriström-Larsson born 1953	1982	1981 cooperative project	Jigsaw-puzzle pieces in sawn and painted wood mounted in the ticket hall.
DANDERYDS SJUKHUS (p 220–221)	Hertha Hillfon born 1921	1978	1974	Walls and pillars decorated in ornamental art ceramics. Cement mosaic on the floor with an inlaid serpent—symbol of medical science—in the pedestrian walkway leading to the hospital.
	Pierre Olofsson born 1921	1980	1978	Wall decoration in plaster and artificial stone.
DUVBO (p 268–269)	Gösta Sillén born 1935	1985	1978 open competition	Fossil-like relief patterns in the rock face transforming into sculpted forms. The lighting stresses the relief effect. The platform colour contrasts with the brown-grey cave.
FARSTA CENTRUM (p 182–183)	Gunnar Larson born 1925	1982	1980	Three-dimensional aquarelle, "Transformations in the Sky".
FRIDHEMSPLAN (p 236)	Ingegerd Möller born 1928 Torsten Renqvist born 1924	1975	1973	Stippled painting of track walls and platform walls. Objects connected with the sea.
GÄRDET (p 193)	Karl Axel Pehrson born 1921	1967	1967 personal commission	Fantastic beetles in showcases.

Hagsätra. *Hammarbyhöjden.*

STATION	ARTIST	YEAR	SKETCH	DECORATION
HAGSÄTRA	Britta Simonsson-Örtenholm born 1911	1960	1956 open competition	Wall decoration "The Flautist" in stone mosaic in the ticket hall.
HALLONBERGEN (p 250–253)	Elis Eriksson born 1906	1975	1973	Motifs from "The World of Children". Various figures and texts against a white background. Painted wooden sculptures.
	Gösta Wallmark born 1928	1982	1981	Supplementary barrier.
HAMMARBY-HÖJDEN	Tom Möller born 1914	1958	1957 personal commission	Brick decoration "The Goat" in the ticket hall.
HJULSTA (p 280)	Birgitta Karlsson-Thorsén born 1943 Ove Thorsén born 1945	1975	1973 open competition	Three pictures (family portraits).
	Olle Magnusson born 1948	1975	1973 open competition	One-picture "Last Harvest in Norra Botkyrka".
	Eva Nyberg born 1943	1975	1973 open competition	One (colourful and critical) picture on several panels.
	Magnus Rimling born 1940	1975	1973 open competition	One picture on three panels (photographic enlargement of a pencil drawing).

Hjulsta. Birgitta and Ove Thorsén: Family portraits.

Mariatorget. J Granit: Sketch.

STATION	ARTIST	YEAR	SKETCH	DECORATION
	Christina Rundqvist-Andersson born 1940	1975	1973 open competition	One picture (bird chart).
	Ruth Rydfelt born 1926	1975	1973 open competition	Two pictures (urban motifs).
HORNSTULL (p 196–197)	Berndt Helleberg born 1920	1964	1961 open competition	Hand cut and glazed Dutch tiles, rod-shaped —with figures in "musical rhythm". Wrought iron gates at platform level.
		1979	1979	Filling gap left by discontinued news stand. Wrought iron and glass.
HUSBY (p 256)	Birgit Broms born 1924	1977	1975	Lime-green cave with light grey, deep blue and minium-red features. Continuous, long picture band with archipelago motifs.
HUVUDSTA (p 260–261)	Per Holmberg born 1950	1985	1978 open competition	A fantasy in colour and shape giving associations with hanging gardens. Decorative patterns on the platform.
KARLAPLAN (p 192)	Tor Hörlin 1899–1985	1967	1965 personal commission	Ceramic decoration of the platform wall.
	Larseric Vänerlöf born 1950	1983	1982 work creation scheme	"That Day and That Sorrow", a 96 m long photographic montage depicting events in Sweden during the 20th century.
KISTA (p 254–255)	Lars Erik Falk born 1922	1980	1975	Sculpture made of painted aluminium profiles.

Liljeholmen.

Medborgarplatsen.

STATION	ARTIST	YEAR	SKETCH	DECORATION
KRISTINEBERG	Carina Wallert born 1952	1988	1987 work creation scheme	"Traveller with Animals". Group sculpture in concrete and bronze.
KUNGSTRÄD- GÅRDEN (p 224–231)	Ulrik Samuelson born 1935	1977 1987	1975 1978	Bare rock face, green sprayed concrete, patterned terrazzo floor, cast sculptures from the Makalös Palace, petrified waterfall, painted harlequin arabesque on the roof.
LILJEHOLMEN	C A Lunding born 1929	1964	1962 personal commission	Concrete frieze with shallow reliefs in the ticket hall.
MARIATORGET (p 194–195)	Asmund Arle born 1918	1964	1961 open competition	Sculpture "Man and Pillar" in bronze on platform
	Karin Björquist born 1927	1964	1961 open competition	Golden-brown ceramic rods in deep relief on all inner walls at platform level.
	Kjell Abramson born 1923	1979	1979	Filling gap left by discontinued news stand. Ceramic wall with a low relief in vegetation patterns.
	Britt-Louise Sundell born 1928	1964	1961 open competition	Gate in iron.
		1987	work creation scheme	This station serves as an art gallery. Pictures can be changed, and up to eight artists can be represented.

Ropsten. Hjorthagen exit.   *Skanstull.*

STATION	ARTIST	YEAR	SKETCH	DECORATION
MASMO (p 202–203)	Lasse Andréasson born 1924 Staffan Hallström 1914–1977	1971	1970 personal commission	Paintings on metal mesh at platform level.
MEDBORGAR-PLATSEN	Gunnar Söderström born 1931	1979	1977 work creation scheme	Painting on pillar and metal-mesh wall.
MIDSOMMAR-KRANSEN (p 198)	Anna Flemström Stina Zetterman Hans Nilsson	1979	1978 cooperative project	Midsummer wreath of wood hanging from the roof, walls in low relief.
MÄLARHÖJDEN (p 201)	Margareta Carlstedt born 1934	1965	1961 open competition	Enamel painting "Ebb and Flow" in sheet metal on the track walls.
MÖRBY CENTRUM (p 222–223)	Karin Ek born 1944 Gösta Wessel born 1944	1978	1974	Shadow painting of rock contours in pink, blue-grey and white silicate paint. Corrugated sheet-metal screens on the back walls of the escalator shaft. Work on rock tunnels is portrayed in ten pictures.
NÄCKROSEN (p 248–249)	Lizzie Olsson-Arle born 1926	1975	1973	Motifs, paintings and objects linked with near-by Näckrosdammen ("Waterlily Pond") and the film studios: quotations, aphorisms, stills etc.

Skärmarbrink.

Slussen. Aston Forsberg: Grill.

STATION	ARTIST	YEAR	SKETCH	DECORATION
RINKEBY (p 272–273)	Nisse Zetterberg 1910–1986	1975	1973	Rust-red background. Gold mosaics depicting finds from the Viking period. Pictures of birds, and a "sun" hanging from the roof.
	Sven Sahlberg born 1909	1985	1984	Supplement, following sketches by Nisse Zetterberg and carried out by Alf ten Siethoff.
	Lennart Gram born 1910			
RISSNE (p 270–271)	Madeleine Dranger born 1943	1985	1978 open competition	History book in the form of a time axis stretching from the pyramids to the present day. Detailed texts and maps depict developments in such areas as technology, science, history, religion and art. Light, bright colours.
	Rolf H Reimers born 1938			
ROPSTEN	Matts Jungstedt born 1924	1980	1977 work creation scheme	Gate with leaf pattern in art forging. Mural.
	Roland Kempe born 1907	1971	1969	Painting "Wriggling Snake" on the platform wall and paintings alongside the moving walkway.
RÅDHUSET (p 232–235)	Sigvard Olsson born 1936	1975	1973	Sandstone-coloured cave. Architectural and other objects associated with life on Kungsholmen in bygone days.
RÅDMANSGATAN (p 186–187)	Sture Valentin Nilsson born 1924	1983	1979	Enamel work dedicated to August Strindberg.

STATION	ARTIST	YEAR	SKETCH	DECORATION
RÅGSVED	Björn Selder born 1940	1983	1982	Mobile sculpture "Bird Green" in bronze, fixed in place seven metres high.
SKANSTULL	Gunnar Söderström born 1931	1980	1980 work creation scheme	Paintings on pillars and in the pedestrian walkway, also clowns painted onto metal plates.
SKOGSKYRKO-GÅRDEN	Hans Bartos born 1944	1975	1975 work creation scheme	Wooden sculptures in the form of a gigantic table and chairs on the platform.
SKÄRHOLMEN	Ulf Wahlberg born 1938	1988	1982	Series of pictures on the track wall, featuring different stages of daylight in a landscape with wrecked cars.
SKÄRMARBRINK	Carl Magnus born 1943	1988	1985	Ornament in patinated bronze, the height of a man.
SLUSSEN (p 180–181)	Aston Forsberg born 1922	1964	1962 personal commission	Grill in iron and concrete dividing the platforms.
	Aston Forsberg born 1922 Birger Forsberg born 1922	1966	1961 open competition	Deep relief, "Entry 70 öre" in white marble concrete in the ticket hall at Hökens gata.
	Sune Fogde born 1928	1965	1961 open competition	Mural in enamelled sheet metal and artificial stone in the pedestrian passage at Hökens gata.
	Harald Lyth born 1937	1983	1980	"Derailed", stained glass painting in the ticket hall.
	Gun Gordillo born 1945	1987	1985	A sound-dampening wall, 90 m long and 4.5 m high, has been built at the Slussen terminal, with artistic treatment using neon, patinated copper, rusty iron, cast lead, black Swedish granite and plexiglass.
SOLNA CENTRUM (p 242–247)	Karl-Olov Björk born 1936 Anders Åberg born 1945	1975	1973	Painted motifs on the theme "Sweden in the 70s" depicting the rural areas, pollution, the Hagalund district etc against a green, red and black background.
STADION (p 206–209)	Åke Pallarp born 1933 Enno Hallek born 1931	1973	1972	Paintings linked with sport and the Stadium, in bright colours against an epoxy background.

288

STATION	ARTIST	YEAR	SKETCH	DECORATION
STADSHAGEN (p 237)	Lasse Lindqvist born 1924	1975	1974	"Variable" sporting motifs painted on corrugated aluminium sheets.
		1976	1975	Supplement.
		1985	1985 work creation scheme	Supplement.
SUNDBYBERGS CENTRUM (p 264–267)	Lars Kleen born 1941 Michael Söderlundh born 1942 Peter Tillberg born 1946	1985	1978	Sculptures on the platform walls representing house frontages from the past, and also the future. Supplementary paintings on the track walls. Silhouette composition in terrazzo and high relief depicting an ear and a nose at the bottom of the escalators.
T-CENTRALEN (old part) (p 170–174)	Lasse Andréasson born 1924 Staffan Hallström 1914–1977	1964	1961 open competition	Mural "Clouds and Bridges" in ceramic material at the SL-Center in the Drottninggatan ticket hall.
	Oscar Brandtberg 1886–1957	1957	1956 open competition	Patterns using clinker plates in the Drottninggatan ticket hall, staircase and lower platform area
	Siri Derkert 1888–1973	1957	1956 open competition	Pillar on the upper platform level, with concrete gougings.
	Erland Melanton 1916–1968 Bengt Edenfalk born 1924	1958	1956 open competition	Mural on the track wall, upper platform level, using glass prisms in various colours, non-figurative pattern.
	Jörgen Fogelquist born 1927	1957–1962	1956 open competition	Mural in Spanish tiles in the Vasagatan ticket hall.
	Berndt Helleberg born 1920	1957	1956 open competition	High relief in cement mosaic on the black pillar on the upper platform level.
	Tor Hörlin 1899–1985	1965	1964 personal commission	Murals in structural clinker in the pedestrian passage leading to Vasagatan.
	Signe Persson-Melin born 1925 Anders Österlin born 1926	1957	1956 open competition	Murals in white clinker with decorative figures in ceramic material on the track wall at the upper platform level.

STATION	ARTIST	YEAR	SKETCH	DECORATION
	Egon Möller-Nielsen 1915–1959	1957	1956 open competition	Moulded stone benches on the upper platform.
	Vera Nilsson 1888–1979	1957	1956 open competition	Pillars with stone mosaic and glass mosaic at the upper platform level.
	Britt-Louise Sundell born 1928	1964	1964 personal commission	Gates in art forgings in the passage leading to Klara Church.
	Torsten Treutiger born 1932	1957	1956 open competition	Black and white clinker slabs with varying decoration in low relief on pillars at the lower platform level and in the Drottninggatan ticket hall.
T-CENTRALEN (new part) (p 175–179)	Per Olof Ultvedt born 1927	1975	1974	Painted blue creepers and flowers against a blue and white background, also silhouettes of workers in the Järva line section of the station.
	Ola Billgren born 1940	1975	1974	Paintings in the pedestrian walkway (withdrawn 1984). Eleven portraits of Christ.
	Jan Håfström born 1937	1975	1974	Paintings in the pedestrian walkway (withdrawn 1984). Nine acrylic paintings (three triptychs).
	Olle Kåks born 1941	1975	1974	Paintings in the pedestrian walkway (withdrawn 1984). Twelve paintings.
	Ulla Wiggen born 1942	1975	1974	Paintings in the pedestrian walkway (withdrawn 1984). Five paintings.
	Carl Fredrik Reuterswärd born 1934	1984	1981	Enamel decoration on both sides of the 100 m long pedestrian walkway.
TEKNISKA HÖGSKOLAN (p 210–213)	Lennart Mörk born 1932	1973	1972	Paintings and mathematical shapes and sculptures on technical themes symbolizing the development of technology.
TENSTA (p 274–279)	Helga Henschen born 1917	1975	1973	Theme: "A Rose for Our Immigrants", "Solidarity and Sisterhood". Flowers, the world of immigrants, animals, plants, quotations in various colours against a white background. Wood sculptures. Ceramic birds.
THORILDSPLAN	Huck Hultgren born 1931	1975	1975 work creation scheme	Polychrome sculptures—bench and sun in wood.
UNIVERSITETET (p 214–215)	Pär Andersson born 1926	1975	1973 personal commission	Paintings symbolizing spring and autumn against a blue and green background.

STATION	ARTIST	YEAR	SKETCH	DECORATION
VRETEN (p 262−263)	Takashi Naraha born 1930	1985	1978 open competition	Japanese aesthetics in strong forms. A fantastic composition with sky-blue cubes and white clouds in groups. The pattern seems to emerge from the walls and roof.
VÄLLINGBY	Casimir Djuric born 1941	1983	1981 work creation scheme	Concrete castings transform the pillars on the platforms into gigantic trees.
VÄSTERTORP (p 199)	Jörgen Fogelquist born 1927	1982	1980	"To the Pole with the Eagle": murals depicting Andrées journey to the North Pole by air balloon.
VÄSTRA SKOGEN (p 238−241)	Sivert Lindblom born 1931	1975	1973	Ceramic decoration on a grey cement background, terrazzo sculptures (a male profile 18 m long).
		1985	1984	Supplementary decoration of the third platform.
ÖSTER-MALMSTORG (p 188−191)	K G Bejemark born 1922	1965	1961 open competition	Sculptures in wood on the concrete pillars in the hall at Birger Jarlsgatan.
	Siri Derkert 1888−1973	1965	1961 open competition	Pressurized concrete blasting on the track walls and inner walls in the platform area. Figures depicting the struggle for freedom and women's rights.

Thorildsplan.

Östermalmstorg. Birger Jarlsgatan exit. K G Bejemark: 9 o'clock.

Artotheque

Since 1976, over 100 artists have painted individual pictures which have been collected to form an artotheque. At present, the pictures are used to decorate the walls alongside the track at the Gärdet and Skärholmen stations, and the intention is that they should also be used in three other stations.

The Mariatorget Gallery

Since 1979, pictures have been hung on the track walls at Mariatorget. So far, they have been a random selection from the artotheque described above, but the new policy will be to display a larger selection of paintings from the works of fewer artists—in other words, to develop further the idea of a station acting as a gallery.

The eight artists showing at the Mariatorget Gallery since April 1987 are: Lars Arned, Joachim Granit, Helena Gräslund, Bengt Håbro, Leila Karlsson, Ulf Lodin, Frank Rylander and Eva-Maria Sjölin. All eight were trained at the Stockholm College of Art. Their pictures will be exhibited for at least eighteen months, after which they will be replaced by a new group of artists.

Bibliography

Ahlgren, Magnus, Tunnelbanestationen Vällingby Centrum. Byggmästaren/*Arkitektur* nr 1/1956.

Byggmästaren/*Arkitektur* nr 1/1953, Tunnelbanan i Stockholm.

Arkiv för dekorativ konst, Nytt samhälle ny kultur, en utställning om Siri Derkert. 1979.

Castleman, Craig, Subway Graffiti in New York, MIT 1982.

Dufwa, Arne, Stockholms tekniska historia. Trafik, broar, tunnelbanor, gator. 1985.

Hyman, Bernhard, Coping with Graffiti in New York City Transit Authority Stations. (Anförande vid American Public Transit Associations konferens i San Francisco 1980.)

Konst och Kultur nr 3/1949.

Larsson, Yngve, Mitt liv i Stadshuset. 1977.

Mass Transit nr 9/1979, New York, A Look Underground.

Millroth, Thomas, Rum utan filial. 1977.

Mörner, Stellan, Konst i väntsalar. *Konst och Kultur* nr 5/1946.

Ohlsson, Jan och Ryding, Lars, Vägvisare till konsten i tunnelbanan. 1979.

Sandström, Sven, Stensman, Mailis, Sydhoff, Beate, Konstverkens liv i offentlig miljö. Sveriges Allmänna Konstförening, publikation 91. 1982.

Sandström, Sven och Sundén, Marie Louise, Tunnelbanekonsten och allmänheten. En undersökning vid T-Centralen (Järvalinjen), Tekniska Högskolan och Solna Centrum. 1981.

Sidenbladh, Göran, Planering för Stockholm 1923—1958. 1981.

Stockholms läns landsting, Stockholms tunnelbanor 1975. 1975.

Stockholms stads gatunämnd, AB Stockholms Spårvägar, Stockholms tunnelbanor 1964. En teknisk beskrivning. 1964.

AB Stockholms Spårvägar, T-banan i ord och bild. 1964.

Trafikens Konstnämnd, Stockholms läns landsting (red Jacob Westerlund, Kerstin), Järvabanan, konstnärer i arbete. 1975.

— Kungsträdgårdens tunnelbanestation. 1977.

— Tunnelbanestationer på Täbybanan. 1978.

— *och Arkiv för dekorativ konst,* Bilder och rum under jord. Tre decenniers konst i Stockholms tunnelbana. 1981.

Station Vällingby

Photo Credits

Index

Stations